The Claim of Language

The Claim of Language

A Case for the Humanities

Christopher Fynsk

University of Minnesota Press
Minneapolis · London

An earlier version of "A Politics of Thought: Gérard Granel's *De l'université*" appeared as "But Suppose We Were to Take the Rectorial Address Seriously: Gérard Granel's *De l'université,*" in *Heidegger and the Political,* ed. Marcus Brainard, *Graduate Faculty Philosophy Journal* 14, no. 2/15, no. 1 (1991): 335–62.

An earlier version of "Acts of Engagement" appeared as "Derrida and Philosophy: Acts of Engagement," in *Jacques Derrida and the Humanities: A Critical Reader,* ed. Tom Cohen (New York: Cambridge University Press, 2001), 152–71. Reprinted with the permission of Cambridge University Press.

Published by the University of Minnesota Press
111 Third Avenue South, Suite 290
Minneapolis, MN 55401-2520
http://www.upress.umn.edu

Library of Congress Cataloging-in-Publication Data

Fynsk, Christopher, 1952-
    The claim of language : a case for the humanities / Christopher Fynsk.
        p. cm.
    Includes bibliographical references and index.
    ISBN 0-8166-4481-0 (hardcover : alk. paper)—ISBN 0-8166-4482-9
(pbk. : alk. paper)
    1. Philosophy. 2. Humanities—Philosophy. 3. Language and
languages—Philosophy. 4. Granel, Gérard, 1930– *De l'université.*
5. Education, Higher—Philosophy. I. Title.
    B29.F96 2004
    001.3—dc22
                                                2004008525

Printed in the United States of America on acid-free paper

The University of Minnesota is an equal-opportunity educator and employer.

12 11 10 09 08 07 06 05 04   10 9 8 7 6 5 4 3 2 1

Contents

Introduction: Toward Fundamental Research in the Humanities

Early in 2001, well before the events of September 11, a young student originally from Afghanistan came to me to inquire about a major in comparative literature. Her principal goal was to complete her preparation for medical school, since she and her sisters were planning to open a medical clinic in their home country, but two courses in comparative literature had confirmed that her greatest intellectual pleasure came from literature and the arts. She wondered whether it would be possible to pursue a dual major.

As one may well imagine, my thoughts about this encounter evolved considerably over the subsequent year. How would this student (as much American, by education, as Afghan) be affected by the media's representation of the American undertaking in Afghanistan? How would she confront the new uncertainties facing her? But the initial significance of the meeting also stayed with me because it had prompted me to rethink my aims in undergraduate teaching. The strength of my response to Farhat Ghaznawi's inquiry derived not from her estimation of the value of literary study in relation to her obligations in other scientific fields (that evaluation normally saddens me, for I know it is largely a function of the impoverished character of introductory work in the sciences). Rather, it came from a renewed clarity regarding my sense of why the humanities are so important. This clarity, I must emphasize, came as a kind of reflection of Farhat's vision of her future. Whatever might become of her project, her commitment was genuine and profound. Medicine was no mere duty for her, even if she felt it was not her first love. I was certain that her interest in comparative literature held a related passion (if not the same one). Thus, in response, I was inspired to say: "My job will be to help you to see how your study here will make you a better doctor."

When I speak of "fundamental research in the humanities," I refer generally to inquiry that leads us to reexamine the meaning of notions that are always in question in the humanities. These are, first of all, notions bearing on the nature of being human: birth, death, freedom, desire, community, and so forth. Then there are notions that are fundamental to the respective disciplines of the humanities and frequently cut across others: the nature of art and its place in society, the burden and meaning of the "fact" of history for all social existence, the constitution of the symbolic order and the institution of law, the grounds of "meaning" itself, and so on. When I told my student that study in comparative literature would help make her a better doctor, I meant that she would be encountering far-reaching questions about human mortality, about the social construction of health and the relation to disease, and about the ethical relation that lies at the grounds of community—a range of topics she would have little exposure to in her premed program. I also thought about the aesthetic relation itself (in a very large sense) and how this would contribute to the nature of her experience in Afghanistan. In short, I was considering that the fundamental inquiry we pursue in comparative literature was vital to whatever professional future lay before her and that "vital" meant something very different from "applicable" inasmuch as such inquiry was already *presupposed* in the very foundations of medical knowledge and practice and necessary for any discovery of the meaning of that practice. An answer like the one I gave her could have been given to a student devoted to legal study or to work in human rights, indeed, to any student pursuing a true vocation, for each vocation draws in some way upon the fundamental notions to which I have referred, whether it reflects upon them or not.

Fundamental research in the humanities, as I understand it, intersects with all fields of inquiry and practice—not in the traditional manner of philosophy (may the queen rest in peace!), but in a more immanent fashion that I will be discussing throughout this book. And it does so as research that is specifically *of* the humanities, as research that proceeds from the media to which the institutions of the humanities attend, and in modes of inquiry that differ from those of the positive sciences. In this volume, I will refer to those media generally as "language," normally intending thereby not only language in the limited sense defined by linguistics but also the visual image, the bodily gesture (as in dance), or the media of new technologies. But whatever the form of the media, I will assume (or this will be my argument) that work that is *of* the humanities proceeds *from* the media and insistently *at the limits* of the media that belong to the domains that hold its concern. It is from this "ground," and in the specific modality it helps define, that the humanities truly open to the kinds of topics I have enumerated. It follows, as I will try to show, that these topics (being human, the constitution of symbolic meaning, the human relation to the earth, and so on) must be handled as something more than themes for discussion.

My principal effort in the essay "The Claim of Language: A Case for the Humanities" is to defend the claim that it is possible to speak of research that is specifically *of* the humanities in the way I have just suggested. I focus on the conditions of fundamental research in the humanities, in a philosophical mode, and seek to offer a set of possible paths. I do not claim that the humanities can only be thought along the lines I trace, or that all valid work must return to its foundations and produce a thought on language.[1] I merely try to show that it is possible to describe specific forms of research as properly "humanistic" (a term I will rarely use, for reasons I discuss later), and point to the important questions that open from the basis of this understanding of the humanities. I have no reason to exclude other work normally associated with this designation from bearing its name.

Indeed, a looser understanding of the term seems not only appropriate from an institutional perspective (here, at least, I am a pragmatist) but also necessary. Again, I will be offering only one possible account, and I welcome the thought that there are others. In fact, I hope to trigger their response. But I believe that it is crucial at this time to argue that *there are* humanities and to demonstrate that these forms of research deserve sustained support. In recent years, it has become increasingly difficult to make this claim in anything but a vague or dogmatic manner, and I would argue that this difficulty is adversely affecting the state of the humanities in the contemporary academy and beyond. There is an immense amount of creative work and reflection occurring outside the academy and the system of education. Art and literature are in no danger of expiration. But in that space where reflection on the humanities must compete for limited resources with other forms of research, a possible justification of the name of the humanities is crucial. And there can be little doubt that the fortunes of the humanities in higher education are also reflected at lower levels of the public and private systems.

So my intention is not polemical, for the most part, or exclusionary. It is philosophical. And on this basis I want to offer one distinction. Fundamental research, as I understand it, is not synonymous with theory, if by the latter we understand an application of some conceptual apparatus to a putative object such as the literary text, the visual image, the historical archive, or culture in general. In the forms of teaching and research I want to describe, no such object can be simply assumed, and no "metaposition" is available from which to so treat an object. A very different kind of relation, a more engaged and immanent one, is implied. I try to sketch this relation throughout this book. Here let me assert simply that fundamental research must question the structure of representation. This is an old story, but a failure to pursue this subject rigorously has helped to allow a gradual drift in the humanities toward discursive practices that deny in their very form an access to the questions that should distinguish the humanities. This drift is most troublesome in projects that claim (often superficially) theoretical inspiration, as in some forms of cultural studies. Often political or critical in intent, and governed by an instrumental understanding of theory, they tend to foreclose the very possibility of thinking the political. The latter task cannot be pursued, in my view, without a consequent and ongoing questioning of the structure of representation.

Fortunately, theoretical practice has begun to move away from the formalism of schools that gripped it for so many years (the construction of theoretical camps concerned essentially with reproducing their own language, however much they claim to be addressing a "real"). At least, this has been my impression. But it is not clear to me that theory, in the domains of the humanities at least, has advanced very far in undoing an obvious dissociation between its languages and the existential concerns it claims to address. It has not advanced far in drawing forth the *matter* of its concerns—what the Greeks called the *pragma*. There is no escaping formalism, to be sure; it haunts every use of language. But a great deal of the most important philosophical and theoretical work of the past century attempted to think and write its way through this challenge, developing forms of discursive usage that were in no way reducible to the traditional form of the concept. These efforts are crucial to what I want to name "fundamental research in the humanities," and I will return to them later. Here, I will observe simply that fundamental research diverges from much theory in that it is always seeking the limits of its language in responding to that to which it seeks to answer: those dimensions of experience and symbolic expression that summon it (as a kind of exigency for thought) and to which no concept will ever be quite adequate. Such research is impelled by its own neediness and its sense of being answerable, whereas theory, governed by the concept, proceeds with ever-expanding appropriations; fundamental research proceeds from *encounter* (always from a sense that something has happened to which it must answer), and it seeks encounter. In theory, there are no encounters.[2]

In the wake of these statements, let me anticipate two possible objections to my undertaking. Some readers may feel that a return to philosophy of language and issues of an ontological or existential cast marks a kind of regression in view of the profound transformations in the field of literary and cultural study of the past two decades: the opening to globalization and to a host of attendant sociopolitical issues, the opening to new media, and so on. My response to this concern is that I am seeking the means to address these transformations in a way that honors what the humanities have to offer. The challenges such transformations represent are indeed part of what calls for the humanities, and it is the task of fundamental research to help find forms of response. I am reminded here of Paul Celan's words near the end of his famous "Bremen Address," devoted in large measure to his efforts to write in and after the murderous events of the Second World War. He suggests that his thinking may perhaps accompany the efforts of the generations of poets that follow him: "Efforts of those who, with man-made stars flying overhead, unsheltered even by the traditional tent of the sky, exposed in an unsuspected, terrifying way, carry their existence into language, racked by reality and in search of it."[3] Fundamental research, today, begins from this sense of exposure, this groundlessness. It is a world-historical condition that has only grown more severe in the forty-six years since Celan made his statement, for the ascendency of a technical determination of being on a global scale has grown more apparent every day. With these words, I do not mean to give a solely negative cast to the challenges facing the humanities. And I refer not to technologies per se—the new media, for example, represent an exciting challenge to thought and to the imagination—but rather to the expanding sway of technicity (or what Heidegger called *Technik*) and the forms of technical reason that devolve from it.[4] But I stress this issue of technicity because it suffuses every sociopolitical issue that might become a concern for the humanities. I need hardly enumerate the social and ecological afflictions that ravage the contemporary world by reason of the intimate bond between technicity and capital; nor need I dwell, I believe, on the despair that grips many of those who seek effective response. I would only add that this despair is fueled in important measure by a sense of the abstract character of social agency, and I would include this abstraction on the list of afflictions. It invades all dimensions of life in our societies of discipline and spectacle—all social relations and all affective experience. One way of understanding Celan's phrase ("to seek reality"), therefore, is to find ways to respond *concretely* to these forms of affliction. It is not simply to produce a "better" theory (that "enlightened" assumption has shown its limits); it is to find new ways to think agency and to give theoretical responses a genuine force.[5] There can be no single, true way. Surely we have learned at least that lesson. But I will argue that the humanities are critical to any search for real paths, that we must learn from those who "carry their existence into language."

Other readers may find my argument a little too philosophical for their taste. One colleague told me he thought I was wielding an awfully large hammer for such a small nail. I suppose that I disagree with regard to the size of the nail. The failure in much contemporary theory to achieve the level of reflection I am proposing for the humanities has contributed to blocking significant access to the questions I see as crucial to any effort to rethink their nature and role, starting with the question of the human. I am not demanding that reflection in the humanities move to a new level of complexity or difficulty; I am suggesting only that it cannot ignore the ontological dimension of language and the existential questions that open there. I cannot see why humanists should find a meditation on the nature of language an irritating complication. And it is crucial to establish today that a renewed reflection on essence is not a regression for the sociopolitical concerns of contemporary thought (an area where the term "identity" still holds sway).

I would add that I am inclined to appeal to the history of thought and a rigorous approach to its texts a bit more than is fashionable today because I believe that such an approach is the condition for any discovery of the creative dimension of philosophical practice. A respect for the history of thought is one form of resistance to the market forces at work in the field of contemporary theory. But in a more positive light, it is also a means for disclosure (as I try to demonstrate in this volume with reference to the modern history of speculative thought on language). As for careful reading, my work is predicated on the notion that one cannot begin to approach the *poietic* dimensions of the texts of philosophy, or the realities at stake in that practice, without sustained attention to the grain of thought in its textual elaborations. And I would even add (but now I risk becoming really unfashionable) that I understand attentive reading as a means to preserve important dimensions of the text of philosophy for the work of future scholars—that is, for a futurity I cannot represent as my own. I understand it, therefore, as a kind of service. But "preservation" does not mean "monumentalizing"; philosophy comes alive only in the act of translating and carrying over that forms the substance of tradition. Only in this sense of tradition can philosophy become *thought*. In arguing for "fundamental research in the humanities" and in practicing it, however modestly (I cannot claim to meet fully the ideals for which I am arguing), I am working for the possibility of thought in the academy. An uphill battle, to be sure, but I believe that the possibility of dwelling in the "ruins" of the university, and of doing so with integrity, depends on this effort.

Two Precedents: On the Practices of Philosophy

I have joined to my principal essay on the humanities two essays devoted to the university and the politics of critical thought, essays that carry forward concerns that have marked my research since its inception. Because the two essays do not immediately prepare the argument of my title essay and even risk conflicting with it in certain respects by reason of the way they are embedded in their respective occasions and problematics, I have grouped them into a single part. (The reader who is eager to get to the topic of the humanities can skip directly to Part II, "The Claim of Language: A Case for the Humanities.") My hope is that these two essays will indeed be read as precedents but in a sense that stresses the dimension of time. Still, there are important continuities, and since these essays address the larger question of the university and the evolving task of philosophical thought, they may serve to broaden the context of my meditation on the humanities and suggest its larger import.

The first contains a reading of Gérard Granel's *De l'université*. No essay has been more important to me over the past fifteen years or has occasioned so much internal struggle. The initial version outlined a kind of deconstructive politics for philosophy in the midst of the Heidegger affair. (This was a time when a phrase such as "deconstructive politics" could still have some bite.) Its arguments seemed entirely necessary to me as they were elaborated and then appeared immediately faulty. It took me almost a decade to articulate for myself why the critical stance I entertained in that paper was untenable. When I did so, however, I realized that I had been struggling with the very notion of critique and the assumptions of most of the critical practice directed to transformation of the academy. I recognized that a different relation to practices of teaching and writing would be required if academic work were to bring to language and practice a real ethicopolitical exigency. Granel had called for such a thing, but his stance remained caught in gestures of flight and refusal vis-à-vis his representation of the global forces of capital and what Heidegger named *Technik*. It seemed to me crucial to develop a freer, more affirmative stance, even while honoring the advances Granel and others had made in post-Heideggerian and post-Marxist critical thought. I eventually found this possibility in a meditation on philosophy of language whose fruits appear in the third essay.

But while I have turned from Granel's critical stance and its goal of clearing space for a university to come, I have not abandoned his ambition of finding ways to anchor intellectual work in its existential conditions (the finitude of human existence, thought always in a relational manner), and thus of combating the increasing abstraction of contemporary existence in this time of globalization. Granel's utterly uncompromising statement of that goal remains thoroughly admirable to me, and I am thus moved to republish my presentation of his work.

A different impetus prompts me to republish, as my second chapter of this volume, an essay on Jacques Derrida's efforts on behalf of the Collège International de Philosophie. Originally commissioned for a volume intended for the Cambridge Companion series, it indirectly addressed the issue of what it might mean to "accompany" Derrida via a meditation on his efforts to strengthen the institutional presence of philosophy in the French academy. My particular interest in Derrida's initiatives concerned his remarkable proposal that a thought of *"destination"* be placed at the heart of the new Collège. In presenting an edited version of this essay, I do not mean to call for a repetition of Derrida's gesture (I want to avoid any exclusive reference to an individual text or school of thought). But his initiative helps demonstrate the point that a *fundamental* rethinking of the nature and task of critical thought is possible and necessary. My own effort in this respect takes a different tack by proceeding from a thought on language, but it can be linked to Derrida's thinking via Heidegger's recasting of the notion of essence (specifically, his meditation on the locution *"es gibt"*). With a reference to the notion of usage in my essay on the humanities, I mark this point of linkage and underscore another crucial point made by Derrida: that any rethinking of the task of philosophy requires a meditation on the *practices* of philosophy. The latter point is also central to Granel's argument and constitutes the shared concern of their essays. In each case, the necessity of thinking philosophy's passage into new sites of engagement points to the need for rethinking the pragmatics of philosophy.

Let me note, finally, that my title essay is intended as a kind of position paper (though I would prefer to call it simply an opening). It is cast in such a way as to be readable in a single sitting, so there is little space for careful justifications of its assertions. The latter will be found in my previous publications, and I have offered references to them in a manner that I hope will not be too insistent.

Since I am synthesizing earlier work, I must leave unmentioned the contributions of many individuals who have helped make this project possible. I would like to give special thanks, however, to my colleague Brett Levinson, who has endured long hours of discussions related to this project in our weekly trips from New York to Binghamton.

Part I

A Politics of Thought: Gérard Granel's *De l'université*

More than twenty-five years ago, and well before the celebrated Heidegger controversy, Gérard Granel wrote an essay titled "A Call to All Those Having to Do with the University (in Order to Prepare Another)."[1] I understood this extraordinary text (playful, but also highly serious) to be a subversive repetition of Heidegger's proposals in his infamous "Rectorial Address"—an uncompromising deconstruction of Heidegger, in other words, but also a reappropriation of some of the genuinely critical and transformative elements of his thinking. When the controversy ensued, about a decade later, it seemed to me time to repeat the call, in an essay on Granel titled "But Suppose We Were to Take the 'Rectorial Address' Seriously."[2] Disturbed by the construction of this controversy in the media and by a timid response from many who had drawn heavily from Heidegger's thought in their careers— "continental philosophers," in particular, but also literary theorists—I felt that a challenge was in order. But the gesture proved naive and just as untimely as Granel's. As I should have anticipated, the so-called affair was no context for a serious discussion of Heidegger's political engagements and their implications for contemporary thought, let alone his ambitions for the university and his attempt to reverse what he termed "the technical organization of the faculties."

Another decade later, Bill Readings undertook a project on the university that would prove to have a very significant reception, though he did not live to see this response.[3] It seemed to me time once again to return to Granel's "Call." But I discovered, in doing so, that I would have to drop the mask he had provided for me and interrupt my relay of his appeal. For I had taken Readings's questions to heart and had begun to ask whether it was in fact still possible to look to the university (even a university to come) as *the* privileged site for an engagement of the question of existence in its ethical and political dimensions. The latter assumption now seemed to me to be burdened with a legacy of critical thinking that had to be left behind—a legacy (stemming from the Enlightenment) that some of the very best thinking about the cultural role of the university has perpetuated through a notion of critique that has reached its historical limits. If the university was to remain our concern (and this was a sentiment I still shared), then new paths would have to be found.

I want to suggest how I came to this conclusion. My aim is not to straighten the record (my relation to the work of Granel can hardly hold general interest in itself), but to address what I take to be a critical issue in the politics of philosophy. Or perhaps I should say that my aim is to speak to the very possibility of a politics of philosophy in a time when its political meaning has dissipated along with the political itself. I have always understood Granel to be undertaking precisely such a project (hence the strength of my early assent and my ongoing engagement with the text), but I have come to recognize that the language in which he cast this project and the revolutionary posture he assumed led to an impasse. Since this language and stance are shared by a considerable number of critical voices in the academy, the implications of the questions I want to raise should extend well beyond my immediate reference. But let me begin by reviewing Granel's founding assumptions and his extraordinary proposition for the preparation of a university to come.

Granel's meditation on the university, and on the possibilities for a critical practice that would maintain the liberatory potential of its idea, is founded upon something he describes in *Traditionis Traditio* as "an absolute confidence in thought."[4] His initial assumption, unaltered throughout his work, is that the efficacy of contemporary theoretical work rests on its capacity to seize the meaning of its history in the tradition of thought marked by the contributions of Kant, Hölderlin, Hegel, Marx, and Nietzsche— a tradition that was gathered together by Husserl and "delivered to its historicity" by Heidegger. The contemporary theoretical enterprise, Granel argued, could be characterized by its attempt at a general inscription of the totality of knowledge (this was in the context of the growing force of the projects of Foucault, Lacan, Althusser, Deleuze, and Derrida). But it could only realize its ambition, he declared, if it was prepared to become both "fundamental" and "ontological" in the senses of these terms developed by Heidegger.

In Anglo-American critical discourse we are not accustomed to see the antifoundational discourses, generally referred to as "poststructuralist," characterized in such a manner. But it should be recognized that Granel's statement of confidence in the possibility of such a fundamental turn for modern theory essentially reaffirmed similar statements made by Derrida regarding the project of deconstruction, whose scope Derrida declared to be nothing other than "the greatest totality—the concept of the *episteme*,"[5] and whose enterprise he considered ubiquitous. "No exercise," he wrote in *Of Grammatology*, "is more widespread today, and one should be able to formalize the rules."[6] This is not the deconstruction discussed in literary and philosophical departments in North America, but it is what immediately caught the attention of one of the most distinguished French philosophers working in the phenomenological tradition, and it became the basis for much of his future work. A philosophical thought embracing the totality of knowledge is possible, he declared, and *differently* possible than in the metaphysical tradition.

But "differently possible" meant for Granel that thought could no longer proceed from a center located in the texts of the tradition and instituted as fundamental philosophy. It could not be a matter of establishing a new governing center where a notion of difference or even "writing" would replace a determination of Being as presence. A deconstructive reading of the history of ontology would be crucial to the project he was undertaking (where else, as he put it, could one obtain a working knowledge of difference?), but this project could not inhabit the established space of philosophy and assume philosophy's traditional, over-arching position in relation to the sciences. The practice of thought would have to pass out of the instituted space of philosophy and into a series of articulations with other discursive practices (the multiple, material sites of meaning). Philosophy's proper object would thus have to be what Granel termed the "practical finitude" of the various orders of discourse. It would be a matter of opening the theory of any given discursive practice to thought, and thus to its ontological grounds, but only in a movement that would never transcend that practice, except to remark the free-dom that presided at the act of its foundation. To couch this in the simplest terms: every scientific practice rests on a determina-tion of the being of its object that is immanent to that practice but unavailable to it as long as it remains within its thematic limits. The task of thought, as Granel understands it, is to make the turn by which this foundation is dis-covered, but always in and from the site of the discursive practice in question.[7] Being *is* nowhere other than in its pragmatic articulations, and the task of thought, in Granel's view, is to engage the pragmatics of Being by reworking the various discursive modes in and from their institu-tional sites and material comportments.

The task of thought, once again, is a reworking. The word Granel uses is *reprendre*—literally, to retake or recapture. But while Granel's very militant version of fundamental philosophy might lead us to look to the term's military connotations, *repren-dre,* as he uses it, actually hails from the language of knitting and mending. "Every discourse knits with its power to speak," as Granel says in a beautiful little essay published in *Critique,* and philosophy "reworks the various practices by loosening or tight-ening the stitching of their 'nothing' [their articulation of Being's difference from itself], which is to recognize the latter as the very material of all practice, there being no practice that is not 'philo-sophical.'"[8] What he terms somewhat allusively a "nothing" here is indissociable from what I referred to above as the fundamental of a discursive practice, be it mathematics, the study of language and symbolic forms, economics, anthropology, history, physics, or any other. Once again, this foundation does not subsist apart from these practices in a domain that philosophy could claim as its own, but must be drawn out *in and from them* through the incursion of thought. It is the task of thought to render to them their always singular philosophical possibility, to discover their practical finitude. Granel phrases the task this way:

> If the non-positivity according to which thought "proceeds" remains what for want of a better word we will continue to call "ontological," and if its role remains "fundamental," it still does not repeat the effort of a fundamental ontology, which dominates a series of regional ontologies, all of it "accounting rationally" for the work of science and all practices. There is no "domain" of the fundamental. There is, however, a fundamentality for every (real) domain which cannot be regained from within it, so that without the disruption of thought a practice will inevitably remain buried in itself and incapable of shaking off a metaphysical limit, itself the source of various ideological exploitations, of which this practice has only a distant sense, or even no suspicion. But if it is true that this fundamentality of every domain presupposes actual practice, instead of being producible as a subordinate part of a (supposed) general knowledge "of" the fundamental, it is also true that this fundamental, determined and undetachable from its writing (or from its procedure), reinscribes each time a certain form of Being "itself" (as difference)—though the invocation of Being, and above all, in an "itself," is here a reference to *nothing* (to nothing that subsists as an ultimate signified or as any thing at all). Thus, the epagogic coming and going of thought, in its courage, presupposes *at one and the same time* a knowledge "at hand," immediate and therefore effective, of the positive domains, and an entirely different knowledge (which would probably be impossible to acquire otherwise than through a working-over of the Western metaphysical corpus, in other words, through work "at the center"), that is to say, the knowledge of the differing of Being and of its fragility, the knowledge of a

general form of healing-over (under its *smooth* aspect of "meaning" or "ideality") of a general form of wound. Which is not to say that there would be anything like a "general wound," unless it is in the form of life, of the mortality of life.[9]

I have cited Granel at length because I can hardly think of a more arresting statement of the critical task imposed by a thought of finitude. But I do not want to linger too long over the seductions of its rhetoric, because it is important to emphasize that this description of the "epagogic" movement of thought has concrete referents. It captures very precisely, for example, the opening movements of Derrida's *Of Grammatology,* specifically Derrida's deconstruction of Saussurian linguistics and his playful construction and deconstruction of the idea of a science of grammatology.[10] This is not the place for a lengthy discussion of deconstruction, but I would note that if I insist a bit in this evocation of Derrida, it is in order to bring home with a familiar example the point that the thought in the name of which Granel eventually entertained a critical transformation of the university was intimately related to the philosophical movement that took as its "non-object" of reflection the structure of writing that Derrida himself termed at one moment "the common and radical possibility of the sciences." Granel saw no reason why such a critical practice, which was already underway, already accomplished at a specific site, could not be generalized and thus form part of the basis of his initiative with regard to the university.

Before turning to his political elaboration of this project, let me underscore what I take to be a crucial element in this thinking, its existential component, using this term as does Heidegger when he speaks of the "existential analytic." This dimension of his thought appears when Granel emphasizes in the methodological statement I have cited that such a general critical practice could never be the work of one subject alone. A thought of practical finitude implies that Being can only be thought from the determinate sites of its inscription (even if a general knowledge of the event of inscription is required to think its very singularity). Philosophers must rework the text of their tradition, but the path of thinking prescribed by Granel requires that they engage another practice. They must be philosophers (philosophy must speak for them in some essential way), but at the same time they must also be, for example, poets or mathematicians. They must *be* poets or mathematicians, Granel insists, which means that they find in the language of their field a concreteness that answers to their experience of being in a world (is this not what takes an intellectual into a particular domain?). Granel does not attempt to set "reasonable" limits to the number of times an individual may make such passages through the straits of the different discursive practices, but it goes without saying that each of us has our limits, and since there is no one domain of the fundamental, the limits to the possibility of carrying out fundamental critique are principial, not empirical. The practice of thought is a practice of the limit—a passage to the very limits of the languages that constitute a multifold and discontinuous space and time of meaning. No one subject can pretend to traverse the multiple orders of language.

Thus, the contemporary practice of philosophy presupposes an irreducible multiplicity of subjects and something like a community of thought. For if it is still the whole of existence that forms the (impossible) object of philosophy[11]—its matter, its *Sache*— then community becomes an exigency for it. Not the hermeneutic community of conversation or dialogue (working always from or toward a common ground of meaning), but rather a multiple effort at drawing forth and exposing this "whole" that historizes in being-together *(Mitsein)*—an effort that must always take singular forms precisely because this "ground" of existence gives itself in no other manner and occurs nowhere else. "The totality is in no one's hands," Granel writes, and by this he means in the grasp of no one subject.[12] No subject can name it, produce it, or speak for it in any adequate fashion (as defined by the metaphysics of representation). But the world remains the concern of each Dasein—its *pragma*, its affair—and since *it is at stake in every practice* (every time this practice begins to work at the limits of its language), it is in no other hands. Philosophy, therefore, names the turn by which this fundamental political reality would be brought forth in and for each discursive practice, and by which something like a common cause (for the world is irreducibly *shared* in being together)[13] might be exposed. Once again, this cause (the whole of existence) could never be taken up except in renewed initiatives at particular discursive sites, each one remarking the finitude of its articulation of the historical provocation to which it has answered (a provocation known in need), and calling, thereby, for further initiatives. The communication of this call (as in a malady or a passion: the exposure of the fact that political existence is at stake in each discursive practice will inevitably spread the need for further initiatives) would lead to a continual, generalized transformation of the fields of knowledge and the institutional structures that serve them.

From even this very rapid sketch, one will recognize that the pragmatics of thought Granel envisions is both ethical and political in character. "We must grasp as political," he writes, "the decision to discover, formulate and accomplish the possibilities of being of the singular/plural Dasein."[14] Such a "political" act does not entail seeking and imposing a new representation of political reality on the basis of some theoretical position. It is not a matter of achieving determinate political counterpositions and eventually some political hegemony. It is a question, rather, of rendering political—making an object of public concern—a dimension of existence that political representations inevitably foreclose *as representations*. It is first of all a matter of rendering political public being itself—that material exposure of beings to one another that is the an-archic site of all political negotiation. What is at stake is thus the very meaning of politicality. As Granel puts it in one of his characteristic flourishes, everything is at stake here, though "everything" is not an object of representation; it is what opens to question when the world comes into question, when human being becomes a question for itself—the very object of genuine praxis (or pragmatics) as Heidegger understood it in his appropriation of this notion from Aristotle. I will cite again from Granel's "Call," this time a statement of Granel's political objectives in the context of the expanding reign of global capital.

"Political power," both the first condition of all serious
action until now and the inaccessible end of an interminable

militancy, and like the "global discourse" to which every [political] organization feels obliged . . . are henceforth no longer objects for us. Or rather, they are taken for what they have always been: "objects" for representation and will—and even false objects, since according to the Kantian lesson, there is no way of thinking the totality under the charge of "objectivity." The world is certainly an existential for Dasein, and certainly a figure of the whole for it, but it is not Dasein's object: it is its pragma. The genre of the whole involved here is comparable only to that which forms for each individual that inevitably missed totality they call their "life," and to whose lack they must try to be adequate.[15]

Granel's gamble in his work on the university is that when thought reaches such a level of reflection, a real engagement with the question of the meaning and direction of the university can occur. And he presumes further that from this fundamental questioning a real process of social transformation can be envisioned. He discretely accepts the notion that a thinking critical reflection must *lead* social transformation, and sees the university as the privileged site for a form of free critical thought.[16] As you can see, we are not so far from Heidegger, at least in some respects.

The fact is that we are both very close and very far away. Regarding the proximity (which concerns assumptions about the relation between the praxis of thought and the possibilities for political existence), we should observe that Granel is actually carrying an aspect of the project announced in the "Rectorial Address" beyond the point Heidegger himself was willing to take it. The "Rectorial Address" dates from 1933; by 1935, Heidegger had abandoned his hope for a general transformation of the structure of the university. I won't try here to untangle the thicket of personal and political reasons for this retreat. I cite only the philosophical one, which is lapidary: the sciences cannot think. Granel, as I understand him, implicitly refuses this judgment for reasons (entirely compelling, I believe) that are Heideggerian in inspiration. The appropriate countercitation to Heidegger's statement would be the one I cited earlier: "Every discourse knits with its power to speak." Every discourse, in other words, engages a determination of Being, and can be opened to the turn of philosophy, or is always already making that turn. So there is no reason to accept Heidegger's claim of 1935 that thought can be the pursuit of only a few, and there would appear to be no impediment, logically speaking, to a deconstructive repetition of Heidegger's rectorial initiative—at least to important dimensions of it. If we couple this latter point with Granel's belief that the university can and should lead social transformation, we can begin to see how Granel really did envision a repetition of Heideggger's move from fundamental ontology to a politics of the university.

And we have good grounds, I think, for growing wary. The problem is not so much the Heideggerianism I have evoked thus far (though, regrettably, I may have induced that assumption by reason of the Heideggerian shorthand I have had recourse to), but rather the retention of the idea, *after the deconstruction of fundamental ontology I have outlined,* that the university could be the central and privileged site for social change. In brief, if it was indeed not a matter of writing difference where metaphysics once read presence, if the thought of practical finitude genuinely points to a notion of irreducibly multiple passages of thought, then it is hard to see how the university could continue as a guiding center for social transformation, even in a new form that has yet to be envisioned. It is as though Granel got caught in his gesture of repeating fundamental ontology, as though he was seduced by the language of philosophy into retaining the idea of the university's gathering and organizing role, even if only as the ghostly site of the nothing (or the evanescent site of freedom) that attends all acts of interpretation or institution, all acts of speech.

I will return to this question after just a few words on why Granel is quite a way from Heidegger. To put this in summary form (because it is impossible for me to do justice to this question in the present context), I would note that Granel seized quite firmly the heart of Heidegger's initiative by grasping how Heidegger had attempted to set a revolutionary concept of philosophical praxis at the foundation of a new university. By "revolutionary," I do not mean simply new (though it was that), I mean fundamentally transformative, and I believe it can be argued that Heidegger understood that transformation to be constant.[17]

So Granel attempted to recover the most radical dimension of Heidegger's thinking while severely critiquing the most regressive, namely, his gesture of identifying a people, the German *Volk,* as the one subject of that revolutionary praxis. Heidegger's reversion to a metaphysical invocation of the will to power of a national subject is what made him a proponent of a conservative revolution. I am passing over, of course, the less "fundamental" but equally egregious aspects of his acts, starting with his complicity with the Nazi apparatus. All of this requires the most severe critical analysis, and Granel, I should emphasize, did not fail to undertake it—well in advance of many of the principal players in the Heidegger controversy. But his most active and critical philosophical gesture, I believe, was to demonstrate the utterly untenable character of Heidegger's appeal to a national subject. He did not just go back into the existential analytic to deconstruct the residual metaphysics in Heidegger's gesture (which was my own initial move in trying to bring forth the significance of the notion of *Mitsein*). He focused instead on the praxis of existence and its subject by reading Heidegger with Marx (following a hint from Heidegger) and deconstructing any appeal to a people or a popular culture that would pretend to escape the disappropriating forces of capital in the era of *Technik*.[18] I cannot go into the details of this analysis (and not all of it is available—Granel's appeal to Marx is the fruit of years of unpublished seminars held in Toulouse), but it is worth noting that it undercut in advance any appeal to cultural or ethnic identity and entailed a thorough critique of the modern notion of production. This is a critique that many who speak after Marx today would do well to study.

One of the important results of that analysis, I believe, is Granel's conclusion that there can be no escape from the modern protocols of production *within* the modern socioeconomic framework, and that therefore no project of reform, of the university or of any other social institution, could serve the political ambition I described earlier. Granel is uncompromising on this point, even more so than Bill Readings, who followed Granel, among others, when he argued that the university could no longer be understood as an essential site of ideological struggle. Readings's assertion that the modern corporate university has lost the cultural role assigned to it at its foundation, namely the formation of the subject of the modern state, is fully consonant with Granel's view that the place of the university in modern society can only be understood now from the basis of the technical imperatives of capital. In Granel's analysis, there can be no refuge from these imperatives through an appeal to a collectivity or communitary existence outside their hold, and there is no point of rethinking the essence of the nation or state, now that the nation-state has become the frame and instrument for the politics of capital and is reducing history to the fortunes of a world market. In Granel's view, there is no escaping the horizon of what he calls "the triply rational language of economy, politics, and technique" from within the structures that serve it. So it cannot be a matter, once again, of political *reform,* at least as this is defined in traditional terms. One must instead reconceive the very meaning of political action in the way I tried to sketch it earlier, and carry the struggle into the order of the symbolic itself. One must disrupt that language at its foundations, and to do so one must find a means of intervening from without.

Now, Granel gives a very radical pitch to this idea by drawing from the language of revolutionary struggle. Listen to his description of what it means to do theory:

> No practicing subject of any modern form of knowledge,
> whether he or she produces it, propagates it, or suffers it, can
> hide from themselves any longer that *schiz* that divides them
> when they enter into the theoretical simulator in which
> develop conjointly the object and procedure of *such* a form of
> knowledge. They can no longer hide it not only because the
> transcendental veil under which was dreamed an (im)possible
> unity of formal knowledge and real habitation has been torn
> to shreds, but more gravely because all modern science has
> entered into a process in which it can only go forward
> ("produce results") by capitalizing itself, in the proper sense of
> the term—that is, by seeming to have become in itself the horn
> of plenty or the miraculous source from which "emanate"
> what it produces and the very work that produces it. Such a
> situation is one in which, from within, nothing can be

changed; it is a situation from which one can only withdraw,
or that must be stopped. From the outside.[19]

That sounds like a call for the reformation of the Red Brigades
or some comparable group. But I am fairly certain Granel would
refuse any such organizations by reason of their inherent complicity with the modern notion of political power.[20] The only
movement that might approach the kind of anarchic interventions
Granel has in mind would be one that resembled the early ACT
UP. In any case, to intervene from the outside is to bring the foreclosed question of existence in a world (human existence in its
materiality and historicity) into the sites of cultural production
in an unpredictable and unassimilable manner—that is, without
attempting to institute that intervention by establishing some
theoretical or political position. It would be a matter of intervening in the symbolic itself, and in a manner that would be more
than merely "discursive."[21] When Granel proposed his "Call," he
was not hoping for responses in *Critical Inquiry;* he was seeking, rather, a disruption of such neutralizing institutions (where
difference is housed and mediated in a carefully controlled "conversation"), and the introduction of a "differend," or multiple
differends. His gang (or "ship of fools," as he designated it in a
delightful piece of theoretical fiction that sketched, near the end
of his essay, "what this might look like") would be a mobile band
of critical philosophers who would emerge freely and unexpect-
edly throughout the university and other cultural institutions with
the purpose of conducting fundamental critique at the sites of intervention. His roving co-conspirators would seek forms of public
action that would expose the different sites of cultural production
to the question of their meaning for the existence of the subjects
that work in them. I cannot explore everything Granel tried to
convey with this extraordinary fictive sketch for the work that
would prepare a new university, but I think one will see that he
was giving a kind of free form (a noninstitutionalizable form)
to a critique that would be multiple, an-archic, and would come
from everywhere and nowhere. His mobile critic would effectively emerge from that nonsite of difference or that absent center that he retained for his notion of fundamental critique. It is

difficult not to applaud, or at least to laugh, when reading this description of Granel's Nietzschean band: it's gay, sovereign, and delightfully intoxicating.

Let me acknowledge, in any case, that I certainly applauded and meditated for quite some time on what it might mean to be party to such an undertaking. But I've sobered a bit after years of attempting to follow the spirit of this proposal in a state university (aspects of it, anyway), and I do not believe that the sobriety is due entirely to fatigue. I have come to sense that there are significant problems lurking in the premises of this joyous fiction. First, it is not clear to me that Granel has quite abandoned important elements of the philosophical ambition that he has claimed to deconstruct and that informed the creation of the modern university in Germany, namely, the notion that the university should serve as the organizing site for a culture's self-representation and reproduction (a notion of the university's role that continues to inform a wide range of critical projects).[22] When he calls upon the history of the university to evoke its possibility as a site of resistance to the destructive forces of capital (its manner of arresting history and suppressing any question of a "world" through the imposition of the technically managed evidency of what is), he turns to a Heideggerian evocation of a people's will and its need for self-foundation.[23] This is not an Idealist or Romantic thought of foundation, and there is no notion of *Bildung*. Moreover, Granel makes it clear that the Heideggerian precedent must be severely revised. But the implicit appeal to a gathering and unifying of forces (implicit, already, in the idea that the university should lead social transformation) inevitably calls up some of the problems raised by Heidegger's own thought of foundation in the 1930s, be it in the realms of thought, politics, or art. Granel is clearly seeking an entirely new conception of the university's "poietic/political/philosophical" role in relation to the forces of global capital, but his appeal to the university's historical meaning weighs heavily on his words. We see this even in the free fiction that conveys the idea of the kind of work needed to clear the ground for a new conception of the university, as I will try to show shortly.

But I want to emphasize immediately that while Granel's proposals seem caught in the tradition's hold, he does not fall into the snare of the concept (represented today in different forms of critical theory). In this respect, the role of his roving critical band is not that of the heroic intellectual described so powerfully by my colleague William Spanos (who envisions a synthesis of Foucauldian genealogy and Heideggerian deconstruction for the sake of a historical and political analysis of the interlocking forces of oppression that define the shape of the educational system). Granel does not hope that a group of such individuals can win the day by the sheer compelling force of their analyses and thereby open grounds of agreement and affiliation. He does not lay that burden on his cohorts because he has no faith in the efficacy of this kind of critical discourse. He recognizes that the academic institution can assimilate and turn surplus value from all such critical labor. There will always be a place in *Critical Inquiry* for the decisive critical analysis of *Critical Inquiry*. Moreover, he recognizes the inherent abstraction of this form of theoretical representation; it cannot reach, in its language, the dimension of existence that must be engaged. So Granel abjures the solution of critique so long as this critique does not find a way to disrupt the structural apparatus itself and its communicative order, that "triply rational language" of modern institutions.

I fully concur with Granel on this last point.[24] But one has to ask, I think, whether his idea of reopening the public space to a new order of discursive relations and a new form of political action from everywhere and nowhere does not risk reproducing the traditional critical model in a kind of rarified form. Isn't Granel still caught in the design of transcendence if he posits thought as *outside* the global horizon of modern capital and *Technik* and can only envision forms of intervention that remain absolutely faithful to the nonsite of their emergence? If the task is to open that nonsite through furtive and multiple interventions that refuse their own institutionalization, to open it in a general manner from anywhere and nowhere, and to gather it, then are we not also, in fact, in the strict obverse of a traditional notion of foundation? True, Granel acknowledges that this action will always be impure, that this attempt at opening a different public space will have to be constantly renewed, that the furtive appearance of this political space will always fade. Moreover, he explicitly claims that we must not turn difference into a new critical center. But I fear that as long as such thinking remains directed by a totalizing construction of the symbolic horizon of the language of capital and *Technik* (as the horizon against which it unfolds), it can do no more than spin off versions of its sovereign, but properly impossible, task, and reproduce endlessly the nonpositive affirmation of its difference from that symbolic order. It can offer no more than a constantly renewed affirmation of the transcendence of thought itself. And if it then seeks to gather this affirmation under the quasi-messianic promise of a future university (even in refusing its representation and deferring indefinitely its realization), it effectively repeats its idea, in however ghostly a form.

Before I go further, I want to be sure I have not created the impression that I do not share something of Granel's confidence in thought (if not an absolute confidence)—an "optimistic" confidence if the latter rests simply in the idea that thought can happen and the question of existence can be engaged, even in the university. I also believe that there is good reason to attempt a general form of critique like the one I sketched earlier. The transversal passages Granel describes should be pursued, and I believe these passages should be attempted particularly in the direction of the social and natural sciences. North American and European universities—but I should undoubtedly say *all* universities—are increasingly serving the technocratic mechanisms of the world market, and it seems to me imperative to question the epistemological models that inform, in a relatively undisturbed way, the standard forms of training in the fields that serve and constitute this technocracy. I believe we must attempt a much more consequent, more far-reaching form of interdisciplinary exchange than has prevailed thus far (who knows, we might even try venturing over to the School of Education). And in any case, we must not imagine that critique that remains within the formal structures of our disciplines, even if they are conceived as broadly as "theory," has any significant purchase in relation to our sociopolitical site. As long as the disciplines remain intact, critical activity, however intensely it is undertaken, will remain an isolated pursuit. Translations must occur if thought is to have any transformative effect, and there is no reason to dismiss such transformations because they cannot be global and are always subject to forms of recuperation.

But the dream that such a critical enterprise can guide transformations of a general or global character at the level of existence in a world (an existential and ontological level) strikes me as perhaps just that: an imaginary construct with potentially debilitating effects. There is no recovering the world (at the level Heidegger defined it) in a general and unifying manner. As Granel himself knew perfectly well, it must not be reinstalled as the new goal of "an interminable militancy." And as long as critical thought projects such a telos, it risks blocking the singular transformations that are in fact the conditions of real movement. Projecting as its goal the overturning of a global horizon from the basis of a commensurate gathering of existential forces, thought cannot possibly dwell in its sites and realize the engagements that are capable of really *communicating* existence in a world. Such an ambition remains beholden to the totalizing designs of critical theory and perhaps even the metaphysical dream of unity.

The force of Granel's joyful fiction of an infinitely mobile contestation derives in part from an aporia he constructs. On the one hand, he has an acute sense that the struggle must be carried out at the level of the world and for the whole of existence; a gathering of critical forces (a multiple, but concerted, effort at practices of thinking and writing) is urgently required for an open and general confrontation with the reign of *Technik* as it is realized by capital. There is the experience of an exigency here—the "absolute" knowledge that possibilities of existence are given to us to elaborate at this time of the accomplishment of the sociopolitical forms of modernity and that their future requires an overturning of this order. On the other hand, he works with a no less acute awareness that such a struggle could never be adequate to what it opposes without assuming forms that would subvert it. How could a coherent an-archy be achieved (necessarily coherent because of the rigor and precision required by the struggle against a not fully coherent, but inexorable, system of forces) that would be adequate to the cause and resist a dialectical subsumption? In what form can one honor the whole of existence (which is exposed only in singular articulations and reducible to none of them) against the totality formed by the horizon of the "triply rational language of economy, politics, and technique"?

The fiction springs from this aporia — the impossible (but necessary) task of honoring the finitude of existence in a political project adequate to its adversary. The fiction, I should emphasize, presents itself as such; what it performs is at least as important as the idea it seeks to sketch. And indeed, in its imaginative verve and with the tint of a Nietzschean menace (for the discomfort of some, as Granel would love to say, and for the delight and encouragement of others), it succeeds in communicating the notions of freedom and public action that are crucial to the critical undertaking he envisions. At the same time, however, it does not take much to read in its extremity a certain desperation and to glimpse in its mobility a kind of flight. The totalizing construction of the adversary leaves the critical project in a negative space.

Is there an alternative? I am in no position to contest in detail Granel's construction of the logic of global capital in the era of *Technik*, though I have a strong suspicion that the totalizing character of this construction betrays a much more mobile, uneven play of forces, and thus innumerable possibilities for movement. There is no denying the vast and insidious reach of the reigning powers in the global orders (and certainly no denying their terrible ecological and dehumanizing effects). But there is also no account of their unity or inevitability that does not repeat the transcendental move of metaphysics (and its abstraction).[25]

In any case, thought must discover and proceed from what exceeds the reach of these forces (starting with the facticity of human existence itself and that exposure of the human that grounds the ethical relation).[26] When this event occurs, everything seems to be at stake, and in a certain sense this is indeed the case (for one moves at that point to the grounds of meaning itself). But this is a singular, finite event that communicates itself, as I have argued, only in and to acts that answer it.[27] It cannot be set up against a global horizon and in view of global transformation without being stripped of its eventful character (and the material relations exposed there). And it cannot posit "becoming everything" *(le tout)* without betraying its own historicity.[28]

I do not want to argue here for any "blindfolding" regarding the forces at work in globalization, and I certainly do not want to abandon the tools offered by critical theory—it is crucial to attempt to seize the logics of what must be fought. I am trying merely to work toward the idea that the thought of the singular event (whereby existence in a world is exposed) can never be commensurate with the globalizing horizon of theory and that a pragmatics of thought must leave that horizon in search of a new thought of community and relation. It would be naive to think we can simply cast off the negative of a critical relation to the dehumanizing forces of capital and the modern society of spectacle. But I do not think that all stances of engagement should be held hostage to that negative relation and the necessity of a globalizing telos. Indeed, existential engagement of the nature I have sketched is not possible from such a horizon and the distance it presupposes from the material conditions of practice; no new site can be created in that distance. The goal of marrying rigorous critique to immanent engagement requires an entirely different stance, one that takes not the negative path of irony, but rather the affirmative one of what some thinkers have named humor.[29] For the purposes of *being-together,* only the latter mode, I believe, may offer an opening, even as it retains awareness.

Granel was actively preparing the ground for a new relation to possibilities of thought within and beyond the academy, but as I have suggested, his work remained in the grips of a kind of flight, a transcending turn that perhaps suspended the possibility of anything more than the most furtive engagement of a questioning "being in common." This flight, once again, was grounded in an acute, and deeply informed, awareness of the appropriative forces of capital; it may well have been thoroughly justified in certain respects. But it blocked, I believe, the possibility of the affirmative stance to which I have pointed. Granel's thought, like so much modern theory, ultimately casts its transcendence in negative terms, even as it casts off on its joyous account of an open-ended questioning. A different stance is required today—one that assumes its inevitable inauthenticity even as it seeks a truth that exceeds the governing sociopolitical conditions. The task today, I would say, is to find ways of drawing forth and affirming being in common in different sites of engagement—*to make it happen,* in other words, and to allow the communicability of this event to constitute a movement, wherever it might occur. The condition of such a pragmatics lies in a liberating acquiescence (a yes-saying) that is more than a simple positive attitude or a lightness, for it must be thought from the structure of experience itself. Heidegger described the possibility of such acquiescence from the grounds of a structure of exposure proper to the human Dasein, and Blanchot inscribed it at the heart of the human relation to language. From there he evoked "the exigency of another relation."[30] The point is to find ways to practice this opening in and of language at the sites of symbolic usage. Still following Granel, I would suggest that the university—in its "ruins"—is a perfectly good site for getting underway (though certainly not the only one), and the first task is to propagate a version of his "call." But this is not to seek a new space of transcendence in waiting for a new university to save us. It is more a matter, once again, of finding new ways of honorably inhabiting the ruins.

Acts of Engagement

I turn here to Derrida's extensive writings on the institution of philosophy,[1] specifically to two essays that issued from his efforts to help create and set underway the Collège International de Philosophie—two founding documents for an institution that helped shape philosophical work in France through the 1990s. I read these essays, "Titres" and "Envois," as companion pieces, though the first, an exposition of the historical and philosophical exigencies to which the Collège would respond, is in many ways preparatory for the statement—the invitation, let us say—that Derrida advances in the second. By reading them together, however, we can appreciate the performative force and the scope of Derrida's propositions in "Envois," or "Sendoffs," as it is translated in English.[2]

"Titres" proceeds from a gesture that is characteristic of many of Derrida's initiatives: an enumeration of the historical signs that call for the initiative in question. In this case, the signs pointing to the necessity of founding something like a Collège International de Philosophie (the conditions that "entitle" it to exist) belong to what Derrida labels "a re-awakening of the philosophical," a new demand for philosophy (of national and international proportions) that cannot be met within the governing institutional frameworks.

This demand for philosophy is in fact inseparable, in Derrida's eyes, from an expiration of the traditional entitlements of philosophy and the institutional structures founded in its name (at least from the time of the creation of the University of Berlin and in the wake of Kant's definition of the juridical authority of "the tribunal of reason"). "The end of philosophy" and the spreading impact of the discourses engaged in thinking that end are among the motifs that constitute what Derrida understands as a set of multiple (perhaps irreducibly multiple) demands for a new philosophical undertaking. "The end of philosophy" counts among those motifs because this closure appears not just under the pressure of philosophical critique, but also by way of philosophy's exposure to events that are beyond the purview of traditional philosophy and require new forms of philosophical engagement. Events such as:

1. A new global configuration of ethical and juridical issues that have emerged with the modern phenomena of nuclear terror, totalitarianism, genocide and torture, urbanization and ecological catastrophe, and world health issues such as the AIDS pandemic—global issues for which the founding concepts of morality and law (already shaken by critiques emanating from philosophy and psychoanalysis) have proven profoundly inadequate.[3]
2. Technoscientific developments that challenge traditional concepts of life and death (as in medical technology) or space and time (as in developments in the media and communication—transformations that alter the very meaning and constitution of public space).
3. A resurgence of religious movements and associated political forces throughout the world that place new forms of pressure on the values of reason or on notions such as democracy.
4. Cultural displacements—transformations in the arts and their material bases, or transformations

in forms of life. Derrida cites in this regard the fundamental challenges presented by feminist thought.

The list can (and should) be extended. "Titres" and "Sendoffs," already powerfully suggestive of the global transformations that require new forms of philosophical response, anticipate Derrida's meditations on topics such as racism, the global economy, democracy, and law (a topic visible throughout the later essays collected in *Du droit à la philosophie*). But my aim here is not to survey Derrida's inventory of the signs that constitute a new demand for philosophy or to seek to complete the list (even if the exercise would be instructive). Indeed, any effort to map or to represent adequately the new situation of philosophy would only reproduce the theoretical drive to objectify and master a field, whereas Derrida's first point, once again, is that the field of transformations that solicit a new philosophical undertaking *exceed the purview* of the theoretical or philosophical gaze as it is traditionally instituted. It is not a matter of an overwhelming range of phenomena, an unmanageable empirical abundance; it is a matter rather of transformations that exceed philosophy's "phenomenalizing" or objectifying potential. Accordingly, Derrida hypothesizes that the synthesis of the many signs to which he has referred—signs that solicit philosophy without being quite *for* philosophy—cannot be accomplished by any established discourse. Their interpretation, he says,

> Traverses and exceeds, though perhaps without disqualifying them, all of the discourses and all of the thematics that pretend to govern [this interpretation], for example, philosophy (under all its forms, in particular philosophy of language, philosophy of history, hermeneutics, philosophy of religion), the human sciences (for example, sociology in all its forms, even the sociology of knowledge; history, even the history of the sciences and techniques; political science or political economy; psychoanalysis; and so on), or the "natural" sciences, supposing that the latter distinction still stands up to analysis. In other words, the charter of such a

college must not exclude this possibility, that the thought that
would prove to be able to measure up to this unity of the
epoch—if there is an "epoch," a unity, and a measure—is
perhaps no longer scientific or philosophical, in the currently
determinable sense of these terms. And in truth it is this
indetermination and this very opening that we designate, in
this context, with the word "thought."[4]

"The horizon, the task, and the destination" of a new Collège
International de Philosophie, Derrida asserts, is outlined by the
demand for such a thought.

I will return shortly to Derrida's "schematic" for a possible
elaboration of this thought. But before turning to "Sendoffs," I
would like to underscore two important and related points made
by him in the light of his diagnostics of the new philosophical exigencies. The first is that the challenge to philosophy's hegemonic
position as arbiter of rational inquiry—a challenge to the entire
"univertical" ordering of knowledge in the space of the *universi-
tas*—obliges philosophy (or the thought that would succeed it)
to entertain an open set of *transversal* relations with emergent
forms of knowledge and their technical elaborations. Throughout *Du droit à la philosophie*, and particularly in "Sendoffs" and
"Titres," we find a call for *translation* and *transference*—multiple passages (of thought) across institutional boundaries and into
entirely new problematics and institutional (or extrainstitutional)
spaces. The collapse of philosophy's traditional overarching position exposes it, as I have asserted, to the necessity of rethinking
its relation to the multiple orders of knowledge and practice. It
must think its implication in these multiple orders even as it thinks
their role in it (the philosophy in medicine, law, or linguistics,
for example, and, reciprocally, the linguistics, law, or medicine in
philosophy), and it must find new forms of engagement with the
transformations in which it is implicated. The latter imperative—
and this brings me to my second point—entails a fundamental
recasting of the theory/practice relation, a new thought of theory,
praxis, and what Derrida chooses to continue to call *poiesis*. The
need for such a recasting—let us call it the elaboration of a new
pragmatics of thought—is occasioned first of all, and as we have

already noted, by technological developments throughout the sciences and arts. To think these forms of knowledge/practice and their solicitation of philosophy, new forms of competence are required of thought; philosophy must rethink technical and artistic performance, and it must rethink its own capacity to engage such performance. It must rethink the "savoir faire" of the multiple forms of knowledge/practice and think its possible participation in those forms (not just its implication, but its capacity for performative engagement).

These imperatives lead Derrida to devote a section of "Titres" to what he terms "performativity." Moving from a discussion of the need for a new thought of the knowledge/practice relation to the topic of the performative dimension of language, Derrida asserts that the new Collège should take the risk and the wholly original step of placing the question and even the requirement of performativity at the heart of its concerns. No institution of research and teaching, he says, has accorded full legitimacy (the right to full exercise and recognition) to the performative character of language. To be sure, Derrida is well aware that there has always been a place in the university for discussion of the rhetorical effects of language, or its "force"; but his argument is that no institution has recognized *de droit* the place of the *event* in the discourses it sanctions—namely, the possibility that those discourses could alter the contract that authorizes them. No institution has sanctioned (and above all, sought) an alteration of the symbolic order it represents—an act of speech, in other words, that would constitute an intervention in the symbolic. Derrida's words are measured on this topic. "Titres" is, after all, an official document of sorts, and Derrida is not one to celebrate naively the transgressive powers of symbolic acts (he knows too acutely the ruses of representation and entitlement). But when he suggests that the first step in engaging a thought of the performative might involve research into its institutional aspect, he is doing more than proposing a novel topic of study—a topic that he has himself developed at some length in his reading of Benjamin (in "Force of Law," to which I will return, and in texts such as "Declarations of Independence"). He is also implicitly inviting the Collège to consider the "exorbitant" foundation of its own instituting acts and the transformations to which its founding charter are subject. Though "Titres" touches only briefly on this question, it seems clear that Derrida believes that the initial step of considering the institutional aspect of the performative should be taken in relation to the institution of philosophy itself, and ultimately because the deconstructive analysis of philosophy's founding acts helps point to a way of thinking *what calls for philosophy* in the transversal movements that Derrida proposes to the Collège, i.e., in philosophy's engagements with other modes of knowledge/ practice.

What does an analysis of philosophy's instituting performative reveal? Derrida sketches an answer in the preface to *Du droit à la philosophie* and in explicit reference to the initiatives outlined in "Titres." Having observed that any "pragmatic" determination of what may be defined as "philosophy" requires a concept of the essence of the philosophical, and, reciprocally, that any determination of that essence of an "originarist" sort (as in Heidegger) must presuppose a performative "act of language" that marks philosophy's inscription in a given language and an institutional and social function,[5] Derrida goes on to observe that philosophy's founding contract is unstable—by law. Citing the opening declarations of "Titres" (a set of questions more than a set of declarations, in fact: "Why philosophy?" "Why philosophy today?" and so on), Derrida goes on to write:

> The whole chapter that opens in this manner will mark the aporia of a community that proposes to found itself on a contract without prior example, a nonsymmetrical contract inscribing in itself nonknowledge and the possibility given at every instant of breaking the contract, of deforming or displacing not only its particular terms, but its constitutional axiomatic or its essential foundations, even up to the idea of the contract or the institution. No doubt, an auto-foundation or auto-institution always proceeds in this manner, as in the origination of states. But the fiction of a constative knowledge and an irreversibility are always there and are structurally indispensable. Here, on the contrary, it is through fidelity to a quasi contract that is absolute and without history, to a

precontractual engagement, that the institutional contract
might be put back into question in its very presupposition,
and even in its essence as a contract. It is always in the name
of a more imperative responsibility that one suspends or
subordinates responsibility to a constituted seat of authority
(for example, the state; but also a given figure of philosophical
reason).[6]

The philosophical engagement is always subject to suspension
by reason of a more fundamental engagement, an always prior
responsibility of thought (a responsibility that is *to* philosophy,
Derrida suggests, but to an always more responsible philosophy,
more faithful to the "promise" of philosophy). Before any instituting act, therefore, but also inseparable from it, is what he
names, in *Specters of Marx,* an "originary performativity."[7] In *Du
droit à la philosophie,* and in reference to philosophy's engagements in relation to the other, he names it a "yes."[8] As we consider Derrida's own performative in "Sendoffs," we will approach
this "yes" and Derrida's implicit suggestion that a thought of
this engagement will provide the path for understanding what
calls for philosophy in the new conjuncture to which the Collège
seeks to respond.

In speaking of a performative in "Sendoffs," I am referring
to the quite forceful and demonstrative gesture Derrida makes in
advancing a proposition for setting the Collège on a path toward
the thought he identifies in "Titres" as "the horizon, the task,
the destination [*destination*]," of this new institution.[9] This *coup
d'envoi* for the Collège is a proposal for a program of research
devoted to the thought of "destination" itself. What does he
advance with this term (which I have translated, somewhat neu-
trally, with its cognate)? It is, first of all, not a thesis, a topic,
or a category, in any of the traditional philosophical senses of
these terms. As a strategic intervention for engaging the limits
of the philosophical itself, it has a more schematic character; it
condenses and formalizes possibilities for thinking philosophy's
engagement of the transversal passages to which philosophy is
called. Derrida evokes, in this respect, its "performing" and "performative" value[10] as a strategic lever for intervening in the current

conjuncture, a conjuncture marked by a singular turn in the problematic he identified in "Titres" as "the end of philosophy." On the one hand, he says, the turn (and return) to philosophy on the part of the social and natural sciences takes the form of a meditation on ends or finality (which, along with the question of "transmission," in all its breadth, forms the basic lines of Derrida's guiding schema).[11] This turn meets in philosophy itself a fundamental transformation of the problematic of ends and transmission in the form of a new thought of "dispensation," "sending" ("l'envoi"), and the gift—a thought that no longer belongs to philosophy proper (construed as ontotheology) and has the force to recast both the history of philosophy as a thought of Being and all the fundamental questions of philosophy and science: the hoary questions of truth, meaning, reference, objectivity, and history (among others).

As many will recognize, an explicit and unembarrassed appeal is made here to Heidegger's thought of the gift and sending of Being, and to everything that follows from Heidegger's gesture of thinking essence in general from the relation he thinks with the phrase *es gibt.* To be sure, these "destinal" relations, preceding and opening the possibility of any relations of predication and communication (all subject/object or "intersubjective" relations), have been subjected to their own recasting in Derrida's thought of the trace and *différance,* and Derrida is quite clear in reiterating that his translation of Heidegger is profoundly transformative.[12] Nevertheless, it is worth emphasizing that Derrida does not shy from taking over the Heideggerian legacy in all its fundamental reach.

Of course, the term "fundamental" must also be subject to a "destinal" reworking (it must be thought precisely from "engagement," from "sending off," from a contracting of relation that is also a setting underway). But Derrida underscores powerfully that the new Collège must not fail to assume it in response to the demand for such reflection emanating from all the sites to which philosophy is called:

Even if we had not been convinced of it in advance, our consultations have provided us with an eloquent proof: the demand for this type of research is very marked today, and it is capable of mobilizing great forces and taking original forms. For reasons and along directions that remain to be analyzed, this "fundamentalist" thought has given in to a sort of intimidation before the sciences, all the sciences, but especially the human and social sciences. It can and should find a new legitimacy and cease being ashamed of itself, as has sometimes been the case over the past two decades. This can be done without regressions and without a return to the hegemonic structures.[13]

Derrida thus returns to the fundamental exigencies to which he answered in entertaining the thought of a "grammatology" in the volume by that name—exigencies that have been largely lost to view in the translation of this thought in the various critical discourses (and even the institutions of deconstruction) in the English-speaking world, but that are perhaps beginning to re-emerge by virtue of the alarming turn in the fortunes of philosophy and humanistic research, at least in the English-speaking academies. For many, it has become painfully obvious that a new thought of the humanities is now required—an affirmative thought of their potential implication (and need) in disciplines throughout the fields of knowledge. Indeed, it is the latter exigency that has prompted me to turn to this particular Derridean performance, this demonstrative gesture addressed to the Collège and to all of those concerned by its mission.

So, what would a thought of "destination" offer to a *collège de philosophie* in this conjuncture defined by "the end of philosophy" and by philosophy's exposition to a set of transformations that do not surrender to the synthesizing hold of the concept? Beyond the challenges to the founding concepts of philosophy and science already enumerated, it offers, Derrida hints, a thought of the conjuncture itself: a thought of the conjunctions and disjunctions that mark philosophy's relation with itself and with other orders of discourse and practice, and a thought of the time of these expositions, a thought of their event. The thought of destination is also, and perhaps first, a thought of another historicity.[14] "Sendoffs," limited by its pragmatic occasion, does not elaborate on the latter motif.[15] But it obviously anticipates the elaborations to come in texts such as *Specters of Marx,* a volume in which Derrida captures the resistance of the time (our time, any time) to epochal summation by way of a meditation on the famous phrase from *Hamlet:* "the time is out of joint." As Derrida might well have said in "Sendoffs," had he sought a less affirmative and engaging tone, the time is out of joint for philosophy (are not the many appearances of Polonius another historical sign of its end?). But Derrida finds in this very disjunctive condition the source of a promise—a messianic and emancipatory promise:

> But with the other, is not this disjuncture, this dis-adjustment
> of the "it's going badly" necessary for the good, or at least the
> just, to be announced? Is not disjuncture the very possibility of
> the other? How to distinguish between two disadjustments,
> between the disjuncture of the unjust and the one that opens
> up the infinite asymmetry of the relation to the other, that is to
> say, the place for justice? Not for calculable and distributive
> justice . . . Not for calculable equality . . . but for justice as
> incalculability of the gift and singularity of the an-economic
> ex-position to *autrui.* "The relation to *autrui*—that is to say,
> justice," writes Levinas.[16]

As we might anticipate, the step from a thought of destination, as Derrida describes it in "Sendoffs," to a thought of justice, as it is evoked here, is a short one. In *Specters of Marx,* it is made via an interrogative appeal to Heidegger's translation of *Dike* in "The Anaximander Fragment" as "Fug," or "jointure." Anaximander's fragment, Heidegger tells us, offers a thought of justice founded not on an economy of vengeance or retribution, but rather on an enjoined or "destined" order or "jointure" in Being, an order whose an-economic gift is attended by an irreducible dis-order *(Un-fug).* Derrida's critical move vis-à-vis Heidegger is to draw out the necessity of this "dis-" and to unsettle, in this manner, Heidegger's characteristic emphasis on a gathering measure in Being. For Derrida, the thought of a necessary dis-jointure in every destined order offers the link to a possible thought of an experience of history that is the condition for the notion of justice he pursues throughout his latest works.

This is not the place to second Derrida's engagement (re-engagement) with Heidegger's meditation in "The Anaximander Fragment" by working through the compelling motives for his critical reading. But I would like to linger just a little longer at this juncture where a thought of destination opens upon a thought of justice. For this juncture is marked, and thought, by Heidegger with a notion that Derrida does not pursue, but that points back powerfully to the motif of performativity that is at the heart of Derrida's proposals for the new Collège and may therefore help us grasp the link (or create a new one) between his understanding of the performative event and his understanding of the interruptive relation that leads him to speak increasingly of a "messianic" experience of justice. I refer here to Heidegger's thought of "usage" — *der Brauch*. *Der Brauch* is in fact the term with which Heidegger translates the "kata to kreon" with which the Anaximander fragment opens. "Entlang dem Brauch," Heidegger offers for this phrase: order and disorder are enjoined according to *usage*. What is this usage? At the level at which it is evoked here (the ontological level, we might say — indeed, Heidegger suggests that we are dealing in this instance with the oldest and most original thought of Being in its difference from beings), it names the interruptive relation between Being and the "there" of its truth. More precisely, and no less technically, it names for Heidegger the interruptive appropriation of the human essence to language, in *Ereignis*, that gives all relation. It is "*the* relation" as Heidegger says in his essay "The Way to Language":[17] the contraction of relation that lies at the origin of the "setting underway" of language itself, and thus at the origin of any gift of language, including its gift of itself or its gift of Being. With his thought of the relation of usage, Heidegger obliges us to think the *es gibt* that Derrida has given us to think so powerfully in recent years, from an *es brauchet*. At the heart of every gift, there is usage.

Heidegger approaches the thought of usage most frequently and most overtly from an implicit rethinking of his early thought of the "essential praxis" of the human Dasein. I would suggest, in fact, that "usage" is the term with which he rethinks the relation between *physis* and *technē* that so preoccupied him throughout the thirties. And I would add that he is rethinking both *praxis* and *poiesis* from the "pragmatics" of usage to which he refers in his Parmenides lectures when he undertakes his analysis of praxis as *Handlung*. In effect, he justifies his translation of *to kreon* as *der Brauch* (he justifies this translating *Sprachgebrauch*) by thinking the term from its linguistic proximity to the Greek *keir* (the hand). Thus he thinks all forms of *praxis* and *poiesis* in relation to a *Handlung* that is an "aletheic" comportment of delivering something to its essence, or according to it what is properly its own (to paraphrase Derrida's own reference to this notion in *Specters of Marx*).[18] But Heidegger insists in all his discussions of *Handwerk* and *Handlung* that human usage must be thought from a prior "use" of the human in *Ereignis* for the destining of Being. Let me try to be precise here, because I mean to mark a dimension of Heidegger's reflection on *Handlung* that Derrida himself, in his superb discussion of the hand, does not address.[19] Heidegger makes it quite explicit that all *Handlung*, as a "delivering" comportment of usage, takes its possibility from a grant (a destining, let us say), that opens within language. All *Handlung*, as Derrida notes precisely, is thought by Heidegger *from* the essence of language and from the manner in which language gives relation in giving itself. So we must think human "usage"—human practice in general—from the *es gibt* of language and Being. But the gift of language presupposes, in Heidegger's analysis, a prior dis-position of the human essence, a prior appropriation to language that is the ground of the subsequent "yes" to language (I mean subsequent as well as prior in a logical sense) by which humankind accedes to the grant of language, its *Zusage* (this is the "yes" that Derrida has made resound so powerfully—a "yes" that redoubles the originary exposure to which I am referring). Once again, the human essence is used, Heidegger says, for the appropriative movement by which language is first set underway in its essence, its *Wesen*. Heidegger's description of this latter usage (he calls it the "er-eignend-brauchende Be-wëgung")[20] is swift, even elliptical—to the point that it virtually effaces the traces it leaves of the interrupted passage it evokes. Nevertheless, it is clear that with the notion of usage, thought at the level of *Ereignis,* Heidegger is thinking the finitude of language itself—the limit (the relation) that is traced in its setting underway. At this limit is a "human essence" that, as mortal, offers relation in its very powerlessness with regard to truth, a "nicht vermögen" that is the ground of the comportment of *Gelassenheit*.[21] Capable of death, as Heidegger said in *Being and Time*, mortals know an incapacity in relation to truth. The task for mortals, as Heidegger suggests throughout his later work, is to recover relation to this delivering usage, this (non)ground of human destination—to assume in a free usage ("a free use of the proper," as Hölderlin said) its originary abandonment or exposure in this *er-eignend-brauchende Be-wëgung*. This "free usage," Heidegger tells us, would be first of all a *Sprachgebrauch* that remarks the double character of the human implication in language, the way humankind is leant to language and lends itself to language (unreservedly—there is no economy here) in an originary assent to a relation always already contracted.

To restate this schematically once again: A "usage" of the human in *Ereignis* lies at the origin of language's gift, in Heidegger's account; the comportment of *Gelassenheit* proceeds from this originary exposure of the human. But Heidegger then adds that language could not give itself ("speak," as he puts it) without a kind of active assent, a listening that is defining for language and already a kind of speaking. Humankind must accede to language's address, in advance, for language to come to the word. Before any speech, there must be a kind of "yes," a "yes" that remarks and assumes the originary exposure, the usage, that is the distinguishing trait of the human essence. A free *Sprachgebrauch* would then assume and countersign the "yes" to language that already redoubles the originary exposure of the human essence that is at the limits of language.

Might this notion of a free *Sprachgebrauch* describe Derrida's acts of engagement? An easy answer is at hand (is not Derrida's philosophical usage among the most free in our modernity?). In any case, we are not far from Derrida's own account of the structure of engagement; with this rapid sketch of the multifold structure of the human engagement with language as it is understood by Heidegger, I have held closely (as I suggested along the way) to Derrida's own "fictive," "quasi-analytic" account of the "yes" in "Nombre de oui," a schematic unfolding of both the originary performative that is the condition of every performative and the repetition (always "free," always forgetfully reassuming) that is necessary to it.[22] But before entertaining, in conclusion, the pertinence of this account for Derrida's own philosophical pragmatics, I want to suggest that the use value of this appeal to Heidegger's notion of usage lies in the way it points to the necessity of thinking the indissociably existential and ontological dimensions of the thought of the performative event to which Derrida points in "Sendoffs." Neither "existential" nor "ontological" are quite adequate here by reason of terminological inertia,[23] but they will perhaps serve to point provisionally to a dimension of experience to which Derrida appeals in *Specters of Marx* in evoking the messianic relation he attempts to think under the name of "justice."[24] By thinking the performative event from a notion of usage, it might well be possible to recover something of the bodily and historical dimensions of the speech act that have evaded most appeals to this concept. Moreover, the notion of usage (involving, as it does, the human relation to language) helps underscore the point that the "mystical foundation of authority," as Derrida thinks it, lies in a relational structure that announces itself or is announced in every performative act.[25] For every performative (at least in the strong sense of this term that Derrida tries to think) proceeds from an originary engagement that is an engagement with language itself—an opening to language that is an opening *of* language. The performative, as Derrida understands it, is always a linguistic "sendoff," and it is always accompanied by an affirmative engagement. Here, in this linguistic event, we have the "silent companion" of every performative act.[26] Here, in the strictest sense, is what *calls* for philosophy, for a translation of philosophy, in the events of discourse and practice to which philosophy is now exposed in the current conjuncture. In every instance of a performative usage, in every performative event (and it is precisely the eventful character of the performative to which philosophy is now exposed), philosophy finds itself potentially addressed with a question of destination and with the dimensions of this question I have tried to elaborate: the question of the conjuncture and with it the question of justice. In every case, there is an engagement with the other, an interrupting exposition.

Will this general account of engagement and address capture Derrida's own acts of commitment, and thereby the conditions for accompanying him? It may well do so in a "quasi-analytic" manner, but it is no doubt essential to respect Derrida's insistence on the singularly ascetic character of the engagement he seeks to affirm in his writing.[27] This asceticism, and the distance from Heidegger (among others) that it entails, is forcefully articulated in *Specters of Marx* when Derrida draws out the disjuncture implicit in all jointure and argues that the "exposition" to which I have pointed in Heideggerian terms (the relation to an "impossible" implied by Heidegger's notion of a human powerlessness) must be understood far more radically than Heidegger ever allowed. It must be understood in and from an abyssal structure of experience that involves a constant ex- or disappropriation. The "yes" to justice or to democracy, proceeding from an immemorial exposure, and projecting or enjoining upon its messianic promise as an opening always possibly to come, unfolds in an ever more arid or empty space, a "desert in the desert," as Derrida says, "a desert pointing toward the other, an abyssal and *chaotic* desert, if 'chaos' describes first of all the immensity, the unmeasure, the disproportion in the saying of an open mouth, in the waiting—or in the call—of what we are naming here, without knowledge, the messianic: the coming of the other, the absolute and unanticipatable singularity of the coming *as justice*."[28] It is from such an experience and such a call that Derrida reads Marx in *Specters of Marx*. Its structure is universal, Derrida argues,[29] but its singular repetition as an inherited injunction[30] bears a distinct signature. It resonates in *Specters of Marx* with the force, the "weak messianic power"[31] that is proper to the "originary performative"—but only inasmuch as it is assumed by Derrida in a new engaging act, a new "messianic" claim.

Derrida "accompanies" Marx, we could say. Might this be a model for the accompaniment sought here in relation to Derrida himself? A model, at least, for the repeating engagement required by any accompaniment in writing or thought? If it can, if perhaps we can accompany Derrida from the basis of an engagement like the one Derrida undertakes in relation to Marx (and the modality of this "perhaps" marks the fact that such accompaniment, when it is given, can never be a certain acquisition), then it remains essential to underscore that such accompaniment cannot be undertaken without the risk of new engagements, new responsibilities. There is the responsibility of discrimination, first of all (accompaniment, like inheritance, requires choice, as Derrida emphasizes in relation to the multiple "words" of Marx). We must be willing to *read* Derrida, not just apply his concepts, cite him as an authority among others, or take his text as an object of scholarship. Then there is the indissociable responsibility of renewed commitment to an other that disappropriates every contracted bond. Few, undoubtedly (at least today), will assume the term "messianic" for this engagement, while others will applaud at the way Derrida has raised the stakes with this *gage*. But the "yes," however it is thought, must be unreserved in its opening to alterity, and it is clear that one cannot predict the paths onto which it may open. We see, therefore, that to join Derrida in thought is to advance toward the possibility and responsibility of a freeing accompaniment—a "sendoff." It is to advance with him to a point of departure.

Part II

Part II

The Claim of Language: A Case for the Humanities

How can we speak for the humanities today? Can we speak in their name to evoke a necessary task for thought?

I raise the first question largely in the context of academic and public policy and from experiences of institutional decline. As an administrator and faculty member seeking to address the health of the humanities in a public university, I have discovered that requests for significant resources are not merely discounted in light of other priorities—they frequently meet uncomprehending or indifferent ears.[1] It is becoming clear that the very existence of the humanities in many universities—or anything more than a token existence—cannot be taken for granted. The situation in state capitals and Washington is more complex and certainly no better. How can a strong justification for the humanities be articulated in the contemporary institutional context?

I raise the second question more as a philosopher, and from a sense of intellectual and ethicopolitical urgency. The ever-accelerating consolidation of technocratic imperatives and the dissipation of political existence have terrible implications for life in North America and on a global scale. The very meaning of modern *experience* and its multifold articulations in differing

forms of life is at stake in the technical transformations underway. From where, if not the humanities, might the fundamental
questions related to this contemporary situation be raised? Are
the humanities not crucial to reflection on the nature of the
human and a host of ethicopolitical issues including the nature of
being-together and relations to the earth? But on what grounds
can one really make this claim for a specific role for the humanities? Does one even rightfully call on something by this name?

It is evident, in my mind, that my two questions are intimately
related to one another. In fact, I do not see why one would seriously raise the first (and fight for an answer) unless one already had
something of an answer to the second, however inchoate. There
is far more at stake here than a few jobs. But I also believe that
one cannot articulate a compelling social role for the humanities
unless one is able to say what the humanities *are*. The fundamental nature of the humanities and their specificity as a site of teaching and research have to be rethought. This task has been avoided,
even sometimes refused, in the contemporary theoretical context.

There was a moment, in the weeks following the events of
September 11, 2001, when a need for renewed thinking on fundamental cultural values, on the meaning and possibility of civic
participation, and on notions as basic as mourning and com-
memoration, or peace and war, emerged unmistakably in American consciousness. This awareness receded dramatically as the
media assumed the national work of mourning, and it quickly
ceded to ideological certainty in the administrative consolidation
(under the name of a "war on terror") of a conservative agenda.
There is little left of the opening that occurred in that remarkable
moment before a shared ethical and civic questioning gave way
to national self-assertion and a demand for unified support for
American military forces. But for many observers at the time,
the emergent need for reflection pointed to a crucial role for the
humanities in public life. Many, as one will remember, turned
to institutions of faith, but there was undeniably a place for the
humanities that was awaiting articulation.

Why did this articulation fail to appear? The forces arrayed
against such a project cannot be underestimated. (Beyond immediate forms of intimidation in that period, I refer to the economic,

technocratic, and disciplinary forces that increasingly paralyze democratic life; one will recall that citizens were urged after 9/11 to resume their roles as consumers). But I am convinced that it ultimately could not appear because humanists were unprepared to say *how* the humanities could realize their role, and thus were unprepared to assert it. The existing assumptions about the role of the humanities in public life and education (their role in the development of cultural self-understanding, ethical and historical thinking, and so on) were largely ungrounded, or grounded in the most shallow fashion.

To be sure, there is a general consensus regarding the ends served by the humanities in North American society.[2] From the basis of this consensus, it is not impossible to garner resources from public and private agencies. But when we approach the fundamentals, the "details," things grow considerably more uncertain. *What are the humanities that they should serve such ends?* How do they serve them, and in what ways do they also define them? Does this "service," or "ends-directed" relation exhaust the meaning of the humanities, or do they answer also to some further calling? What really calls for the humanities, and are they even appropriately called "the humanities" (does that appellation respond to something, or is it, finally, an abstract grouping of academic disciplines and research interests)? One does not have to ponder long over these questions to recognize that few established and widely accepted answers are available, that however voluminous scholarly production might be in the relevant fields today, there is little language available to replace in a compelling fashion a traditional "defense" whose terms have faltered. We could easily conclude that as far as the humanities are concerned, we have witnessed the collapse of a discursive order. And we might well suspect that the gulf between the ease with which we may appeal to the humanities and the difficulty we experience in defining that to which we are appealing has something to do with the sorry state of humanities programs throughout North America.

Do I overstate regarding the discursive situation I have described? We may take the measure of the latter situation by looking back, however briefly, to the 1980 report of the Commission on the Humanities sponsored by the Rockefeller Foundation.[3]

Some would argue, of course, that the report already had something of an anachronistic flavor at the time of its publication (since a "continental" assault on the tenets of humanism had reached North American shores well before). The discursive order that speaks through its language, they would insist, had begun to erode well before the commission undertook its work. The point is undoubtedly correct from a long theoretical point of view, and we may assume that it was even shared by at least a few of the authors who contributed to the report. But what is most noteworthy is the report's tone, the sheer strength of its language, even its verve. If members of the commission knew full well that its language was growing problematic in various registers, they could afford to mute their reservations. The report's language was still publicly viable, and we can hear this fact in almost every sentence, in a confident assumption of humanist verities that is hard to imagine now.[4] Can one find such a confident tone in speaking of the missions of the humanities today, even with a refurbished language that draws on the latest conceptual advances? And if not, or if the appearance of an occasionally strong statement on behalf of the humanities strikes us as such a glaring exception (I think of statements placed on the editorial pages of the *New York Times* in recent years by Agnes Scott College, for example), would we not have to entertain the possibility that the humanities have in fact become a kind of institutional abstraction, an academic entity without any sense of its own internal and historical necessity?

Reviewing academic history of the past two decades, we have a strong basis for the last supposition. Within the disciplines of the humanities, first of all, we find a thoroughgoing critique of the universalizing assumptions that allowed the commission to appeal to a common ground for moral and aesthetic judgment, a kind of *sensus communis* that would speak immediately to the concerns of American civic life. The commission's appeal to the Western humanist tradition for its articulation of the way the humanities would serve a common national culture[5] seems almost quaint in light of the critique of the metaphysical foundations on which it rests and the thorough documentation (in postcolonial studies and in discourses claiming adherence to the notions of diversity or multiculturalism) of its sociopolitical effects, both in America and beyond. And if analysis has left any part of the job undone, the politics of identity has effectively undermined the viability of the commission's language within the academy— for better and for worse. When that language now appears, it does so as explicitly ideological, if not simply reactionary.

Of course, the critique of the universalizing assumptions embodied in the report cannot be understood in isolation from the larger cultural context in which it was pursued. We must read this unfolding critique in relation to the entire range of political forces that set the stage for the "culture wars" of the 1980s and early 1990s in North America. I will not pause to revisit the battle lines here, or the more profound cultural, economic, and demographic shifts of which they were a symptom: increasing segregation in a time of dramatically growing "minority" populations, ever more radical inequalities in the distribution of wealth, an upsurge in religious conservatism, and so forth. The range of national and global factors is vast.[6] I will only underscore a small point that has been insufficiently stressed in accounts of these highly publicized conflicts, namely their impact on the symbolic authority of the academy. Indeed, if they were so highly publicized, it is because their representation in the media served in important measure to delegitimate the academy's authority in cultural affairs, even to displace the academy as the privileged seat of reflection on (and of) the humanities. The cultural politics of a newspaper such as the *New York Times*, for example, are quite revelatory in this regard.[7] So, as we ponder the sociohistorical conditions defining the contemporary fate of the humanities, we must take into account a quite effective assault on the symbolic authority of academic discourse and resultant shifts in the very discursive modalities of academic debate. It is not easy to gauge the degree to which academic discourse has accommodated itself to the displacements in discursive authority to which I have alluded, but the emergence of the "public intellectual" is certainly symptomatic in this regard, and I strongly suspect that this sociopolitical factor has played a crucial role in the shift, within the disciplines of the humanities, to forms of research that would seem most properly situated in the social sciences.

However we assess the latter transformations, they cannot be adequately addressed without consideration of a further, and perhaps more fundamental, dimension of the discursive and institutional contexts in which the humanities find themselves today. I have suggested that the culture wars have had an impact that far exceeds their discursive tenor, that their crucial meaning for the academy lies in the way they have worked to resituate academic discourse in the public sphere. But this effect has also been shaped by another transformation occurring within, and to, the university itself—one that fundamentally alters the possibility of the link the commission attempted to establish between the health of the humanities and the health of Western democracy, and thus any traditional justification for the humanities. The transformation to which I refer was marvelously described by Bill Readings in *The University in Ruins* when he argued that the "idea of culture" on which the modern research university was founded has given way to a notion of "excellence" that lacks any referent beyond technocratic standards of productivity and market performance. A university apparatus conceived more and more strictly along the lines of a corporate entity serving the global movements of capital need pay little more than lip service to the civic issues raised by the commission because it no longer understands itself as serving a national culture. Indeed, the "University of Excellence" can remain sovereignly indifferent to the substance of research undertaken in the name of the humanities (any and all sides of the culture wars can be accommodated, provided they promise excellence), and it need never face fundamental issues— such as the meaning of the humanities for a liberal education—as it allocates resources.[8]

When did academic administrators begin to realize that they need not worry about discursive ferment in the humanities, that even political activism could serve marketing purposes? It was not long ago (perhaps only a decade) that left-leaning scholars in the humanities could attribute their declining fortunes to an ideologically motivated retrenchment. They assumed, possibly quite rightly, that academic administrators considered their work potentially threatening to the university's stability and growth (particularly as initial links were made between critical theory and the claims of minority groups). The response to deconstruction and poststructuralism in the media and from conservative groups, the Heidegger and de Man affairs, even the debates over multiculturalism and political correctness—all of this could nourish the now quaint-seeming assumption that critical thought had an explosive or subversive potential, even as ideological considerations were draining out of management criteria. And, needless to say, scholars steeped in the ideology of the academy have been astonishingly slow to give up this illusion. Trained to believe that true intellectual life is possible only in the academy (often accepting, on this basis, poor economic conditions—if not for themselves, then at least for the students destined to replace them in a system devoted to reproduction), they have characteristically failed to grasp that they are functionaries in an institution whose insertion in the "society of spectacle" and in global technocratic systems evacuates the symbolic purchase of their interpretive acts and their representations of symbolic meaning and social justice. They continue to imagine that they are serving a cultural good in their research efforts in an almost immediate fashion, and that by finding the "best answer" in persuasive theoretical arguments with high visibility, or simply sufficient fame in an interpretive community grounded only in consensus (even here, a latent cynicism with potentially paralyzing effects is held at bay by the assumption that such consensus has some social grounding), they will prevail over what would once have been called their "alienation." In the meantime, of course, their rush to find market success drives an ever-accelerating transformation of the discursive modalities of academic publication and exchange—all of which serves an academic machine whose principle concern is productivity.

Some might be heartened by the notion that the ideological alibi is disappearing as it becomes more and more apparent that market factors are driving the protocols of research and disciplinary formation, not to speak of the attribution of rewards, that success in the academic world is increasingly geared to market success and little more. Disciplinary traditions have allowed an astonishing and condemnable complacency. But such transformations share the demonic trait that they tend to veil their own conditions and the losses that attend them, and thus any possibility of finding a relation to them that would allow for the exploration of other paths. Moreover, I strongly suspect that we have a long way to go before we can drag out the Hölderlinian theme so dear to Heidegger ("In danger, there lies what saves . . ."). After all, the transformations to which Readings pointed are driven by the opening of vast new markets—there are new world orders, new "empires" to analyze, as the *New York Times* eagerly announced (for the humanities!) in an expansive article on the volume by Michael Hardt and Antonio Negri, *Empire*.[9] What would recall to the new generations of graduate students in the humanities the temporalities (of learning, writing, and teaching) and the relation to language that distinguished literary or philosophical study even two decades ago? In general, how would distinctions between the form and modalities of research in the domains of the humanities and those of positive forms of inquiry resist dissolution in the university of excellence and the attendant publishing markets as these domains compete for market share in the spaces opened by globalization?

But let us pause a bit more over a potentially more affirmative understanding of the transformations to which I have pointed. Do we need to cast the directions taken in the humanities today in so negative a light? Do we have to accept that they are so easily reducible to the technocratic transformations described by Readings (whose unfinished diagnosis, after all, is painted in rather broad and simple strokes)? Could we not account for the unsettled, fragmented character of work in the humanities (and the halting character of any apology for it) by pointing to a kind of paradigm shift with multiple facets, one whose results are far from being determined? The critique of the universalizing assumptions of humanism, for example, did more than unsettle an ideological stability in the relevant disciplines—its theoretical force called into question fundamental assumptions about the object of research in the humanities and the most basic methodological certainties. The wave of theory in the humanities *opened* the relevant fields in the most radical way, provoking profound displacements in some quarters, reactive formations in others (continental philosophy, which had a kind of institutional claim to the new theoretical models, took a largely defensive posture and still attempts to protect itself against theoretical corruptions of a "literary" sort). Should we be surprised that the fields of the humanities remain in disarray as theoretical production legitimates an ever-expanding field of research and ever-expanding interdisciplinary linkages? Indeed, why shouldn't distinctions between theoretically informed research in the humanities and work in the natural and social sciences dissolve? Who could blame young graduate students for attempting to link their philosophical or literary inclinations to contemporary issues in world health, human rights, ecology, or economic development? Shouldn't they be applauded for these efforts?

This progressive-minded objection might be pursued in relation to the necessary transformations that follow the turn to issues in multiculturalism, gender studies, and postcolonial studies. How could one expect anything but disciplinary disarray in literary studies, for example, when the ideological formation that guaranteed stable disciplinary structures based on (European) national literatures—the privilege accorded to English literature being the most crucial for the organization of literary study in the American academy[10]—began to fall? Disciplinary inertia has guaranteed that the fall is a slow and painful one; most French, German, and Spanish programs continue to insist that their faculty show the requisite national allegiances. And the pantomime goes on in many foreign-language programs despite anguish concerning enrollments. (The move to affix "studies" to these designations marks an important development, but many of the same factors continue to be in play in many programs.) Yet all the while, it is perfectly evident that the opening of global communications and multiple demands for a more diverse and just representation of cultural production spell the necessity for a fundamental reconception of literary study. How can one justify a small set of struggling literary programs based on national demarcations in a time of globalization? Add to this shattering of boundaries an awareness that some of the most profound critical reflection on modes of representation is being pursued outside the academy (in film and advertising, in architecture and design, in computer research), that political and ethical thought is pursued more in think tanks and some NGOs than it is in the academy, and it should hardly surprise anyone that scholars in the humanities fail to produce a coherent account of their common interests. How could the plethora of new forms of research surrender to any interpretive model that would govern them and secure them as being in some way *of* the humanities (and why would such a thing be desirable)? We do not need the specter of bureaucratization (on a global scale) to account for the lack of a cohesive voice that could speak for the humanities. Indeed, it could well be argued that such an interpretation could only frustrate, when the most pragmatic and promising stance is perhaps rather one of affirmation and a concerted attempt to embrace the new formations, wherever they lead across disciplinary boundaries.

The strength of the last objections is undeniable, and they should be developed much further. I subscribe to them wholly. But I also think they are best assumed if one attempts to hold in question at the same time the meaning and specific possible contributions of the humanities. Indeed, I believe that the latter effort is even imperative if some of the more far-reaching transformations to which I have alluded are to achieve their fullest or richest elaboration. In this case, however, it becomes crucial to regain the question of the humanities in this time when a decline in willingness to address fundamental theoretical questions accompanies a decline in resources. We witness today an increasing inability among scholars in the humanities to state how and why their research is in some way *of* the humanities. Readings focused on the alibi offered by the term "culture," arguing that culture had become an inexhaustible object for scholars in cultural studies (and an immediately identifiable referent) precisely as culture was dissipating as the legitimating horizon for their research. His argument requires more elaboration (and perhaps nuance), but it is undeniable that "culture" has increasingly emerged as a presumed *object* and has receded as a question requiring fundamental research into symbolic formations and the constitution of collectivities. It is this lapse in fundamental questioning that makes the drift toward historicist and positive research in the domain of culture a problematic development for the humanities. For it means that the humanities increasingly lose their capacity to hold open the *question* of cultural and sociopolitical existence (even as they assume in an unquestioning manner the notion that "everything is political"), and gradually fall into a service role in an academy devoted to training students in the management of information. Readings's argument, however reductive or rapid, has the merit of pointing to the way in which the drift toward cultural studies in the humanities serves the requirements of knowledge production for an academy geared to market productivity.

I want to underscore that the current plight of the humanities does not stem merely from an overabundance of possible avenues for research (some of them in conflict) in a time of rapid disciplinary transformation. Their current crisis derives from an impoverishment in their very sense; they have no clear calling in the contemporary university. To be sure, the many just demands for a more expansive approach to ethnic studies in this time of globalization (or for a rethinking of questions as basic as social agency or citizenship) would appear to promise a prominent place to research in the humanities. But the general paucity of questioning as to the very meaning of terms such as "ethnicity" or "agency" condemns the humanities to a kind of theoretical purgatory—the purgatory being increasingly that of theory itself. Again, the question remains: what, in the discourse of theory (the theory of culture, of the social, of the psychic, and so on) *answers* to the humanities; do the acts of thought or conceptualization that theory embodies engage what is truly happening in the phenomena it describes or for which it seeks to account? All too frequently, the answer must be negative. In general, we may conclude that the very *sense* (direction and meaning) of the humanities as a discursive field is unavailable.

To illustrate my point, let me introduce a kind of follow-up to the commission's report, written by and for a private institution. I refer to the "Report on the State of the Humanities at Cornell University," released, to considerable controversy, in the spring of 1998. Although this document was clearly composed for internal purposes and bears all the sensitivities of local strife, we can learn a great deal about the larger state of the humanities and their possible future by following in detail its spirited attempts to articulate a progressive agenda for Cornell that embraces the challenges posed by globalization and technological transformations in the media. The striking de-emphasis of literary studies and philosophy (these areas are hardly mentioned) in favor of transdisciplinary theoretical endeavors and a bold—somewhat obviously partisan—initiative on behalf of the visual arts, which stresses areas like film and digital communication, make it very clear where the report's distinguished authors saw the academic action moving five years ago (and they proved quite prescient). But it must be observed that we will not learn much in the report's forty-six pages about what makes the humanities "the humanities" or how they might best assume their name. The report's "apology" for the humanities stresses only internal institutional considerations (a strong basis for support is claimed on the basis of the distinguished history of the humanities at Cornell), and when it comes time to address what the humanities should be, the report offers only a kind of pragmatic, historicizing project. The authors would like to make the humanities an ongoing *question* by submitting them to the pressures of historical change in this time of globalization, but it is a question framed almost entirely in sociohistorical terms. The following paragraph illustrates this point:

> We urge Cornell to capitalize on its extraordinary institutional diversity by articulating and implementing new configurations for humanistic study in a global age. . . . In particular, we believe that the combination of Cornell's perceived strength in "high theory" (now defined loosely as the study of 18th, 19th, and 20th century European philosophy and thought) and its long-standing commitment to various ethnic and area studies programs makes it a unique site from which to push the limits of theoretical inquiry in the humanities in response to the demands of the times. Because of its wealth of expertise concerning regions and cultures ranging across every continent, Cornell's faculty is well-situated to examine the historically specific circumstances under which the modern humanities disciplines have been constructed, and to analyze and engage the processes through which these conditions have been, or will be, surpassed. Such intellectual work will be crucial in the emerging transnational context of cultural production and cultural critique. Moreover, considered from

this perspective, Cornell's vaunted congeniality to interdisciplinary work takes on a significance beyond the obvious one
of fostering intellectual cross-fertilization and creativity. For
through such region- and boundary-crossing inquiries and the
historicizing perspectives on the humanities disciplines they
may generate, we can promote in both ourselves and our students that critical sensibility and commitment to envisioning
new modes of democratic public culture that should sustain
the University in the decades to come. (23)

It is worth noting that the last sentence of this ambitious
statement contains one of the very few echoes of the Rockefeller
Commission's assumptions about the link between research and
teaching in the humanities and the health of civic life. However
we understand the odd turn that concludes the passage (is the
point really to keep the academic game going?), it is clear that
the echo remains a distant one. Here again, we have a sign that
the traditional definition of the ends of the humanities for civic
life must be thoroughly rethought. Indeed, a significant amount
of work lies ahead if the full meaning of these promising words
concerning the promotion of "new modes of democratic public
culture" is to be brought forth.

With regard to the report's project for the humanities, we are
first confronted with a nod to the critique of Eurocentrism that
has been part of the antitheoretical turn in some areas of cultural
studies. But it is quite clear that the tenor of this passage is hardly
antitheoretical and that it must be read in relation to the constant
emphasis, throughout the report, on the need for a better articulation between theory and positive research, particularly in ethnic
and area studies programs. Indeed, we may surmise that its strong
voice in favor of cross-disciplinary theory played a significant
role in provoking the controversy that greeted the publication of
this statement. Still, it is striking that as the report envisages a
critical examination of the humanities, theory itself appears with
scare quotes. Under the pressure of a new historicizing approach
cognizant of "the demands of the times," it finds itself "high"
like a beached whale. So what theory will advance this project?
The passage tells us that theoretical inquiry will be summoned to

answer to its historical conjuncture while the fields in which this inquiry has flourished are subjected to a rigorous critique of their sociohistorical foundations. This is altogether laudable and vitally important. But how will the theoretical work that undertakes this reflective passage remain answerable to the concerns of the humanities and avoid a metahistorical turn that objectifies them as historically determined formations? We may rightfully assume that the authors of the report are envisioning something more transformative than a sociology of knowledge that finds a new horizon of inquiry in "the emerging transnational context of cultural production and cultural critique." But how can a historicizing critique of the humanities be truly historical if it does not acknowledge the historicity of its object? Unless some definition of the specificity of the forms of knowing and practice that distinguish the humanities is offered, the critique will remain abstract.

Some might respond that an approach like the one contained in the passage we are considering (an approach that avoids attributing essential traits and concentrates on the historical formation of institutions) is salutary. For pragmatic reasons—in both the philosophical sense of contemporary American pragmatism and a political/practical one—"the humanities" must not be reified. But I would have to ask in response: can one speak for the humanities in any significant way without at some point speaking in the name of the humanities and engaging oneself in this name, while defining what is at stake there?[11] In the second half of this essay, I will sketch my reasons for rejecting the pragmatist argument. I will try to suggest why it is possible to speak in the name of the humanities. But I would also like to address the "practical" issue because to accept a pragmatic definition of what counts as the humanities is to cede critical political ground. I would argue that it is to cede the ground of the political itself. I will develop the latter point as I proceed, but to begin, let me follow the report just three pages later as it states its vision for the humanities in a global age:

> The study of global processes opens up new opportunities for collaboration between the humanities and certain types of

work in the social sciences. It is worth considering, for example, whether Cornell should launch a series of research proposals that foreground, specifically, the profound pressures for redefinition and reconfiguration being experienced by the humanities in the era of global modernity, decolonization, and advanced information technology. While it is probable that many peer institutions will continue to use more traditional definitions of the humanities when they apply for external funding, Cornell proposals might, by contrast, seek to provocatively explore the challenges posed by globalization, in its political and technological dimensions, to the humanities as they are instituted at present. Collaborative work with social scientists would be most pertinent to such an effort. Many issues emerging at the forefront of humanistic research today—issues of visuality and virtuality, of translation, diasporic cultures and ethnic studies, mass culture, science studies, and so forth—can be articulated in a relationship to the global that intersects with some strains of contemporary discourse in the social sciences.

I would not want to contest the spirit of this passage. The aims are admirable, and we could undoubtedly unpack in the rapid enumeration of "emergent" issues in humanistic research a sense of the crucial challenges facing the humanities today. But the rest of the statement acknowledges the humanities only "as they are instituted," and nowhere is the question entertained of how the humanities might challenge globalization "in its political and technological dimensions." Might not something of the humanities (conceived traditionally or otherwise) *resist* articulation with "certain types of work in the social sciences"[12]—just as it might resist or escape a sociohistorical construction of the emergence and future of the disciplines of the humanities? And is it really necessary to emphasize that globalization, in its political and technological dimensions, is not a wholly unproblematic affair, that a resistance stemming from the humanities might be of crucial ethical and political import? One might think here of Gayatri Spivak's recent effort to argue for the importance of a new articulation of comparative literature and area studies in light of the leveling forces of development programs undertaken across the globe (programs frequently administered by a well-intended "international civil society" that draws heavily on social scientific research). Spivak recognizes that it would be foolish to oppose such programs, as though one could occupy some "outside" in relation to capital and *Technik* or afford to ignore some of the vitally important functions of these programs. She calls instead for a "supplementing" intervention that would honor idiomatic usages and open to new conceptions of collectivity through acts of imaginative translation.[13] This is an affirmative form of resistance that points toward a new understanding of political practice. For another example, one might think of the criticisms directed at Hardt and Negri's *Empire* regarding the lack of a concrete definition of the term "revolution." Might not a form of thought proper to the humanities help to approach the formidable questions involved in this topic and help to determine in what respects the appeal to such a term is viable? And wouldn't this be one of the points where we meet the limits of collaboration between the social sciences, for example, and the humanities—or rather, the necessity of rethinking them in a transformative manner? I agree with Spivak when she claims that it is the task of the humanities to help us move beyond global political programs (precisely by reason of their programmatic character) toward a thinking that is more planetary in its opening to the many dimensions of human finitude.

As I turn to the central theses of this essay, I will offer one way to define what I have just termed the "limits" of the humanities and social sciences. I will not try to define the humanities *against* the social sciences in any negative fashion, for this could only be counterproductive in light of the many rich exchanges underway between these domains and possibilities to come.[14] I will merely try to mark a boundary in a speculative and questioning mode in order to draw forth something of what I think the humanities have to offer in these exchanges and passages. To approach this site, I want to back up briefly to consider a remarkable aspect of the Cornell report that I noted in passing—the fact that literature passes almost without mention in the review of both the strengths and the weaknesses of the humanities at this major university (which happens to be where I earned my undergraduate degree in English literature and found my vocation). Is this silence due to the fact that the inertia of the disciplinary structure in literary studies constitutes one of the great obstacles to the modernizing program—the transdisciplinary theoretical revision—sought by the report's authors? But then why is literature not itself taken as a kind of ally in this transformation (as years of deconstructive teaching at Cornell have urged)?[15] And what do we make of the fact that there is no significant place given to the study of language? Foreign language study—in which Cornell definitely excels—is urged for its role in answering to the demands of globalization, but the pedagogical benefits are left aside (the fact that ongoing exposure to a foreign language constitutes one of the most important forms of exposure to cultural difference available in college study and an irreducibly necessary step for any responsible research in global issues).[16] Likewise, the exciting proposal for visual studies accords a place to the "image" that would have once been given to "the signifier," but the strong link available to literary study via a meditation on the image as a form of language is left untouched (not to speak of the challenging question of the relation between image and text). The silence on the topic of language is an astounding fact, both with respect to the distance it marks from the founding assumptions of the Rockefeller Commission (the Rockefeller report affirms in its opening pages that the *medium* of study in the humanities is language) and with respect to the history of theory itself. After all, scholars of the first wave of theoretical studies in North America all encountered at some point the lesson that *their material is language* in the most thoroughgoing senses of this phrase. Could this lesson have been forgotten?

Let me say that if we have to do with a forgetting, it is certainly not attributable to some personal lapse in rigor. Nor is it so recent in origin, for it belongs, I would suggest, to a lapse that was *already occurring* with the linguistic turn as it swept literary criticism into "theory" in the North American academy.[17] In North America, as in Europe, the linguistic turn turned right past the thought of language that made it possible (just as it swept by work on language that was flourishing in some North American poetic projects). Only briefly did the question of the ontological dimension of language raised in the wake of authors such as Heidegger and Benjamin (notably by Blanchot, Celan, Derrida, Foucault, Lacan, Levinas, and Lyotard, among others) catch the attention of a few North American theorists and philosophers. The theorists, at least, were poorly prepared to assimilate the philosophical dimensions of the work they were importing (often reducing their implications to a celebration of "undecidability," "paradox," or "impossibility"), and they turned quickly against such fundamental reflection as a demand for political relevance— a demand for a "real" referent—began to shape the theoretical agenda. In their rush to be political, they joined their philosophical cousins in "continental philosophy" in refusing to take the full measure of such fundamental research for the question of politics and for their own disciplinary formations.[18]

To account for this turn in theoretical and philosophical research is to explain, in large measure, how the humanities lost their object (again!) in the course of the transformations briefly sketched earlier in this essay. Or, to put this more precisely, it is to explain why a new "object," other than the positive one offered by work in cultural studies, could not be furnished for the humanities in the wake of the critique of the founding concepts of humanism. Many of the sociopolitical and disciplinary pressures already noted are no doubt pertinent for such an account, as would be an interrogation of the critique of humanism itself, a critique pursued most frequently in a form that neutralized its implications. I do not believe one should underestimate the difficulty of the questions involved or the forms of inertia that prohibit the sheer possibility of taking such questions seriously. Indeed, disciplinary habits have enforced traditional assumptions in such a way as to make it virtually impossible for young scholars to pursue the critique of the metaphysics of subjectivity as anything other than a topic for research. Without the means for grasping their fundamental interest in such research and its broader historical meaning (what might have been called not long ago the possibility of an existential engagement), it is little wonder that more immediately definable sociopolitical exigencies—not to speak of professional interests shaped by the academic market—should draw their attention in the directions I have described.

But behind all of these factors, I wonder if there is not another dimension to the turn from the question of language, a dimension to which Michel Foucault pointed quite forcefully in his famous *Discourse on Language*. I refer here to his argument that disciplinary formations and the social institutions in which they are embedded are organized in part by their effort to contain the anarchic character of language—a potential for disruption (revolution?) that inheres in the sheer fact that discourse can reveal at any moment the inherent lack of stable foundations for the social order and always carries the possible disorder of desire:

> What civilization, in appearance, has shown more respect towards discourse than our own? Where has it been more and better honored? Where have men depended more radically, apparently, upon its constraints and its universal character? But, it seems to me, a certain fear hides behind this apparent supremacy accorded, this apparent logophilia. It is as though these taboos, these barriers, thresholds and limits were deliberately disposed in order, at least partly, to master and control the great proliferation of discourse, in such a way as to relieve its richness of its most dangerous elements; to organize its disorder so as to skate round its most uncontrollable aspects. It is as though people had wanted to efface all trace of its irruption into the activity of our thought and language. There is undoubtedly in our society, and I would not be surprised to see it in others, a profound logophobia, a sort of dumb fear of these events, of this mass of spoken things, of everything that could be violent, discontinuous, querulous, disordered even, and perilous, of the incessant disorderly buzzing of discourse."[19]

Is it possible that behind the impatience with the attention to language required by literary and philosophical study (an impatience that always presents itself as an uneasiness over the uncertainty of returns implied by such an expenditure of time—returns in the form of "results," answers for political and moral choice, or simply remuneration) there is a kind of deep anxiety? Might we not understand the long-standing and pervasive tendency of academics to deny the effectivity of their specific forms of practice in teaching and writing, their rush to find real effects for their work outside the academy (thereby perpetuating an ideological construction of the university's "walls"), as a form of flight from the anarchic dimension of discourse to which Foucault pointed? Is contemporary critical work, in many of its transdisciplinary forms, not in fact participating in what Foucault called "the ancient elision of the reality of discourse"?[20]

So what would it mean to reverse the directions taken in the "linguistic turn" and thereby renew the question of language in a way that speaks to the exigencies of our time? Let us presume that forms of teaching and writing might dislodge the resistance to which I have just alluded and open a form of receptivity to this question (a critical assumption that goes to the heart of what the humanities might be). A first, possible step, then, might be to return to the guiding texts of poststructuralist theory that initially led the latest version of the turn and continue to serve as authorizing references for a considerable amount of theoretical work. An attentive reading of these texts will reveal a thought of language that quite surpasses the simple formulas concerning "the play of the signifier" or "the linguistic construction of reality" that have been endlessly rehearsed in Anglo-American literary and cultural studies. Even the most sophisticated theories of the performative constitution of identity have failed to render this thought, and its reduction in more shallow forms of pragmatism and cultural analysis inspired by psychoanalytic theory and semiotics has reduced theory itself to a remarkably trivial enterprise in many quarters. It is not hard to understand why theoretical research proceeding from linguistic or literary insights should have grown tedious in the past decade.[21] For as its detractors have claimed (though usually for the wrong reasons), a great deal of it was abstract. It insistently foreclosed access to the question of materiality or real experience. Thus the task that remains is to engage the question of language at a fundamental level—i.e., *where a question concerning the being of language opens to the possibility of rethinking notions such as experience, material being, or "the human" itself.*[22] We must restore to the question of language all its ontological weight.

For this purpose, a text such as Jacques Lacan's "The Function and Field of Speech and Language in Psychoanalysis"[23]
would be of considerable interest (not to mention fun), since
it was devoted, already some fifty years ago, to recalling to the
society of psychoanalysts that their proper medium is language.
Unfortunately, anxieties about Lacan's "metaphysics" and his
appeals to mastery (often noted by critics without examination)
have obscured many of the essential points advanced in his work
and probably prohibit fruitful use of it on this occasion.[24] Indeed,
such anxieties attend the evocation of any particular name since
a great deal of contemporary interdisciplinary theory is struc-
tured as a conflictual market where school affiliations replace
thoughtful apprenticeship or accompaniment. Thus, before attending to any particular text (though one *must* attend to singular
textual sites to draw forth the step for thinking that is at stake
here), it is necessary to draw back momentarily and underscore
the basic and essential point that each of the major texts of contemporary theory *share a legacy* that derives from a history of
speculative thought on language that stretches back well over two
centuries. They share this legacy in always singular ways (this is
what makes them such imposing bodies of work), shaping even
the meaning of legacy in their acts of writing. Thus in "sharing,"
we must hear a drawing out and communicating of a historical
relation that is not without division (the French word *partage*
captures this nicely). But the singularity of these magnificent gestures of thought should not blind us to their historical dimension
and to what they share in their elaboration of the question of language. The same point must be made with regard to their prede-
cessors. One may observe in the texts of authors as distant from
one another as Benjamin and Heidegger an astounding convergence in matters of language. How can this convergence be understood except from the legacy they share as readers of Hölderlin
and Humboldt (and perhaps Mallarmé, among others)? Or how
can we understand Wittgenstein's astounding acknowledgment in
1929 of Heidegger's incipient thought on language except from
the basis of a related legacy?[25]

There is undoubtedly more to be grasped here than a series
of lines of textual influence. These authors, like their successors,
answer to a necessity in thought when they reach back to the

speculative history to which I have referred. The linguistic turn, as it happens (again) in the twentieth century, happens to thought; it imposes itself. The insistence of the question of the being of language in the texts of Benjamin, Rosenzweig, Wittgenstein, Blanchot, Lacan, Celan, Foucault, and Derrida indicates clearly enough that we are dealing with something more than influence, and that each of these authors are engaging historical developments in thought that quite exceed their individual acts. Any consequent reading of the poststructuralist movement (and with "reading" I include any use of the relevant texts in new fields of inquiry) must attain the meaning of that fact. One of the intellectual tasks left by poststructuralism is to think the legacy of the question of language that insists so massively in the generative texts of modern theory. A failure to assume that legacy commits theory to practices of representation that are ultimately regressive and cannot resist the market forces sketched in the first part of this essay.

So as I turn now to Foucault's *The Archaeology of Knowledge* to provide an example of the thought of language to which I have referred, I want to emphasize its exemplary character by insisting on its place in a history of thought, a history to which Foucault himself was quite attentive.[26] And to put things a little bluntly: what I want to bring forth regarding the level of Foucault's engagement with the question of language in *The Archaeology of Knowledge* could be repeated in a comparable way for each of the authors whose names I have enumerated in the last pages. I take the risk of reading a portion of this particular text (and thus provoking theoretical argument) because I believe it is critical to demonstrate, from the basis of specific texts, the presence of the latent thought to which I am referring. This latency or unrealized character constitutes the possibility to which I pointed in my introduction when I suggested that this project of rethinking the humanities could never be the only one, but it is nevertheless grounded in a form of intellectual history and thus represents something more than one option among others. I am well aware that I also run the risk of irritating some readers by starting from a formal or technical exposition of what might seem a marginal or even abstract issue (those readers who sense this irritation coming on should move briskly over the next few pages). I will try to suggest quickly how the question of the being of language I want to bring forth is anything but abstract, and that what I seek to draw from Foucault's thought on language marks a kind of threshold for a rethinking of the fundamental issues concerning the humanities. I turn to Foucault in part because this thought is so little appreciated, particularly in those critical quarters that have appropriated his notions of discourse and power for cultural studies and theories of empowerment. Never having been accused of being Foucauldian, I can perhaps use his text as a kind of neutral starting point for the trajectory of questioning I want to pursue (fully aware that such neutrality is impossible, and hoping only for a little maneuvering space in a field where school and disciplinary affiliations are affixed as quickly as possible).

As it happens, the pertinence of Foucault's text for the present occasion extends a little further. *The Archaeology of Knowledge* places a thought of the statement *(énoncé)*, a "pure description of discursive events,"[27] at the heart of a powerfully antihumanist project designed to secure the methodological underpinnings of his groundbreaking work of the 1960s and thus the possibility for future work of a character we would tend to identify today as social scientific. It is hard to imagine a stronger articulation of a possible object for the social sciences than this one. And yet we also find in these pages, almost in relief and at the limits of this "pure description of discursive events," an object that calls for research in the humanities. Here is an instance where a kind of limit between the humanities and the social sciences appears as such, and allows us to envision innumerable points of passage.

I refer to Foucault's definition of the statement as the "elementary unity" of discourse, and thus the proper object of an archaeology of knowledge. The definition is far too complex to examine in great detail, particularly with regard to Foucault's efforts to detach the statement from the hold of grammar, logic, or the linguistic analysis of the speech act.[28] We could say in summary that for each of the latter forms of analysis, something of the statement will always remain as a kind of residue or extrinsic material—a presence of language that is like a material basis for the structures analyzed logically and linguistically, but that exceeds the reach of these forms of analysis. This is a *presence of language,* however, and not a mere physical being. For we do not necessarily find a statement wherever we find a group of signs. A simple assemblage of signs, such as a handful of printer's characters or the letters marked on a keyboard, will not constitute a statement. Yet if those signs are transcribed in some pragmatic fashion (as in the presentation of a keyboard in a typing manual), they will take on the status of a statement. A statement has a unique mode of being, then, that is neither entirely linguistic nor purely material; it is a *function of existence* of signs, that *gives* them as signifying and thus as eventually interpretable. This function of existence constitutes the enigmatic presence of what Foucault terms "the enunciative function," a relational structure that defines (1) the possibility of meaning and truth values, or pertinence (Foucault calls this a "referential"); (2) an enunciative position (which cannot be simply identified with an authorial position); (3) an enunciative field of other statements; and (4) a material existence whose identity and repeatability is determined by institutions of usage.

I refer the reader to Foucault's exposition for the arguments and examples that will make these traits of the enunciative function fully comprehensible. Here, I want to underscore the fundamental cast of Foucault's endeavor. If his "archaeology of knowledge" is concrete, as I noted above, it is by virtue of the concreteness of its object; as we have seen, Foucault has not shied from furnishing his historical pragmatics with an account of the being of language. His pragmatics rests upon a furtive concreteness, to be sure. But then, for such a level of analysis, the meaning of "concrete" must come into question. Here, the being of the statement is defined, once again, as a function of existence that endows it with a "specific relation that concerns itself": "a very special relation" that determines its singularity even as it embeds the statement in a set of relations with other statements in a discursive field and other nondiscursive events.[29] It is something neither hidden nor manifest.[30] Its presence, he writes, "characterizes not what is given [in sequences of signs], but the very fact that they are given, and the way in which they are given. It has this quasi-invisibility of the 'there is,' which is effaced in the very thing of which one can say: 'there is this or that thing.'"[31] To approach it, one must return from the manner in which language refers beyond itself to the presence that dissipates in these signifying movements:

> If one wishes to describe the enunciative level, one must
> consider that existence itself; question language not in the
> direction to which it refers, but in the dimension that gives it;
> ignore its power to designate, to name, to show, to reveal, to
> be the place of meaning or truth, and, instead, turn one's
> attention to the moment . . . that determines its unique and
> limited existence. In the examination of language, one must
> suspend not only the point of view of the "signified" (we are
> used to this now), but also that of the signifier, and so reveal
> the fact that, here and there, in relation to possible domains of
> objects and subjects, in relation to other possible formulations
> and re-uses, there is *language*.[32]

Es gibt die Sprache, Heidegger wrote, pursuing with his notion of the "speaking" of language a material offering of its "fact" that Foucault has all but cited here, but that he can accept only up to that limit that he calls the enunciative level (his refusal of a transcendental turn is as strict as his delimitation of any anthropocentric reference).[33] I have noted elsewhere the strange manner in which Foucault fails to recognize Heidegger's solution to the aporia he describes when he traces this limit in *The Order of Things* and asserts that future thought will have to take the path either of a thought of the being of language or that of the being of man. *The Archaeology of Knowledge* took the path of the being of language; the later reflections on ethics return to the latter path.[34] I believe that there is a kind of necessity to this movement—that the exigencies to which Foucault answered in seeking his "truth," as he named it in *The History of Sexuality* (vol. 2), are linked to an exigency met in any consequent meditation on the essence of language. But on this occasion, I want only to emphasize that when Foucault delimited the field of his research with his "pure description" of the "fact" of language, he effectively bracketed the questions that attend the very possibility of discovering this fact or thinking it (the fact *that there is language* being no intraworldly fact among others to which one might turn one's attention). What involvement with language is presupposed for the offering of enunciative possibilities that Foucault attributed to it and for the thinking practice that would assume it and draw it forth? Surely Foucault himself, if pressed, could not have rested content with the notion that this offering rests in a pure self-relation (if this is how we are to understand "a specific relation that concerns itself"). Language is not a monologue, as Heidegger argued in *On the Way to Language* (though a remarkable number of readers miss this point), nor is its "self-relation" fully described with a deconstructive notion of the iterability of the trace. The fact of language's finitude—it is not an infinite logos—requires a thought of the relation between language and humankind. The opening of speech—every time—presupposes the material site provided by that structure of exposure that defines the essence of human being (at least insofar as we are dealing with human speech),[35] and the problem of thinking that exposure requires a new understanding of what calls for thought and the possibility of thought's answer.

Heidegger sought, for this reason, an *experience* with language, arguing that if the way to language offered by language itself could be engaged with sufficient attention, then this apparent self-relation would reveal a strangeness or a peculiarity that would reveal the human share in the event of speaking and enable a thinking appropriation of it. An offering occurs in language, he said, but this gift and its historical unfolding (the spatiotemporal orderings of *Technik* itself, he argued, must be thought from the way language is given) cannot be thought apart from a usage of the human that it presupposes.[36] The notion of an experience with language, in other words, pointed to a thought of the way the human being, in its essence, is itself given to the speaking of language as a prior condition of this event—not just in the sense that humankind would answer an address of language in such a way as to bring it forth (various references to the interpellation of the subject in theories of the performative constitution of subjectivity touch upon this notion of the way the speaking of language might be engaged),[37] but more fundamentally in the sense that the very possibility of any "saying" in language would presuppose an appropriation of humankind to language. For this contracting of relation, Heidegger proposed the terms *Ereignis* and *Brauch,* notions that ultimately required a more extreme—a more un-guarded—thought of the opening to alterity that Heidegger had once termed "the Dasein in man." We find this thought in the famous essay on *Gelassenheit* when Heidegger asserts that the event of truth requires a kind of powerlessness in the human essence vis-à-vis truth itself; not a passivity or weakness (these notions remain within the metaphysical horizon of a thought of production that Heidegger was seeking to move beyond), but an opening that must be actively assumed—"let be"—in thought.

From such a notion of the exposure that is proper to human being—a finite site of relation to what exceeds finite determination—it becomes possible to rethink the grounds of relation itself. This is an ontological project and an ethical one. If the possibility of relation is thought from an acquiescence, as in *Gelassenheit* (but we might also turn to authors such as Rosenzweig, Levinas, and Blanchot for comparable notions of a "yes" at the heart of human relation), then it is possible to elaborate an affirmative understanding of the assumption of human finitude—a very different stance from ones that seem dictated by the Hegelian articulation of the negating power of thought and the relation between language and death. Of course, these are questions that require far greater attention than I can provide here,[38] but I want to bring home the reach of the questions raised by the thought of language proposed by Foucault (and so many others in the tradition in which he is working). If the thought of the being of language he proposes is carried through in a consequent manner, then it is possible and necessary to pursue a thought of the human that exceeds the metaphysics of humanism. A consequent thought of language, in other words, requires an understanding of what is exposed (and thereby *communicated* in an opening that is prior to any signification, and thus any communication in a standard sense) in those experiences with language where the communicability of language is engaged and brought to the fore.[39] Wittgenstein suggested that the only possible ethical language would be one that brought into play the existence of language itself.[40] I want to carry this thought a bit further by saying that such linguistic events are the condition of bringing the presence of the human to the fore, and everything that is at stake for the fact of this presence (which is nothing less than the ethicopolitical relation). There are some who might prefer to avoid a reference to the name of the human, and I respect their wariness.[41] For my part, I see no need to shy from it as long as we understand the essence of the human as entailing a structure of exposure *where a relation to alterity is immanent.* From here, it becomes necessary and possible to take up the kinds of fundamental questions that psychoanalysis has brought forth in its own attention to origins (that is to say, in its exploration of what is elaborated in primal fantasies): questions concerning the fact of sexual difference, the enigma of the opening of conscious life, and the enigma of language itself (as in the famous Lacanian formulation of the question posed to the subject by the existence of the signifier)—questions that all involve the human relation to a real, as we see dramatically in Freud's case of "The Wolfman." It becomes possible and imperative to think the questions of freedom and human capacity, as well as the nature of bodily experience, or the experience of the earth that Heidegger labored to articulate in his famous essay "The Origin of the Work of Art."[42] And it becomes possible and necessary to think the question of the human relation to the other. For exposure, as Emmanuel Levinas has argued (with Maurice Blanchot), must be thought first from the relation to the other human being; there is no relation to alterity—even the divine—without *autrui.* The implications of this notion for any thought of ethnic or cultural identity are immeasurable, for it means that we must think identity from difference (or from relation). And they are all the more powerful when the thought of a relation to the other is developed along lines such as those pursued by Luce Irigaray in her research on imagination, mimesis, and the ethics of sexual difference.[43]

The paths I have just enumerated are ones I have had the fortune to glimpse and even attempt to some extent—the enumeration is meant to be suggestive, not exhaustive. I would want to include all the paths of questioning that open once the ethical character of the question of language is grasped—i.e., once it becomes clear that every speech event entails at its limits an exposure of the human. We can and perhaps should speak here of the ethicopolitical character of this question if we recall the point from which we started, namely Foucault's meditation on the discursive event (a meditation whose rhetorical dimension—in a larger sense of this term than he uses—points toward his reflections on power). But I do not want to make this a final designation of what I am trying to reach inasmuch as it could have a limiting effect in a contemporary context where the meaning of the phrase "everything is political" is taken to be self-evident, and I believe we must also entertain the question of a relationality that exceeds the political.[44] Let us take "fundamental research," then, to include a reflection that moves to the level of the questions I have tried to open—at the limits of language—and from there assumes the exigencies of a nonfoundational thought; exigencies that emerge for precisely the fact that there is no ground, no logos, for the relational realities at stake in this research. No logos to ground understanding, but a kind of call (Levinas and Blanchot speak of a "saying") that occurs with the exposure of the human.

I noted above that Foucault's delimitation of the object of his analysis of discourse could mark a kind of limit between the social sciences and the humanities. But should not the ground, or (non)ground, of the ethicopolitical relation concern all of the human sciences? Should they not all thereby entertain the question of experience, at least at the level it has been located here (in the exposure of the human to alterity)? But perhaps the boundary remains for the fact that the thought of an experience with language and all of the questions that open from there presuppose forms of research that engage language in a way that remains foreign to social scientific methodologies. To what extent can the social sciences allow themselves to be engaged by the strangeness of a discursive event where language is somehow brought to its very limits and the questions enumerated above (concerning relationality, freedom, mortality, and material being) open to thought? Are such events perhaps the purview of the humanities?[45]

We find such events at those sites that are traditionally the domain of the humanities, of course, and *there are* humanities, we can assert now, because there are sites, occasions, where dance *occurs* as a material event that opens the fundamental questions to which I have pointed, sites where theater occurs, where literature or even philosophy occurs—just as there are occasions when free speech occurs, or moments when a strangely resonant language emerges in a psychoanalytic setting. The humanities are called for by each of those sites, indeed by all sites where a social usage offers itself (as usage) to the questioning I have sketched. Translation is one such site, and I need hardly emphasize the scope of this domain.[46] The humanities are called for wherever the use of language (in the broadest sense) comes into question, or rather becomes a question to itself in the manner of the speaking we have entertained from the basis of Foucault's description of the discursive event.

Maurice Blanchot formulates this event in the "Note" to his magnificent *The Infinite Conversation* in a paradigmatic manner when he offers the following question as a kind of guiding thread for his volume of essays: "What is at stake in the fact that something like art or literature should exist?" This is first a question about the conditions of such a "fact," and thus about language in the broadest sense and the exigencies that lead to a literary endeavor. It then expands as a question for all sociopolitical institutions. For if art, or literature, exists, in all its ambiguity and strange force, what does this tell us about the discursive foundations of any institution and the symbolic order as a whole? A critical task opens here (and again we are at the limits of the social sciences), but also one that requires a response of a more answering character. One could say that to the extent literature exists, there exists an exigency of an ethicopolitical character, or there exists the question of community as it has been developed by Jean-Luc Nancy and Giorgio Agamben. Or there is the question of freedom, in relation to new orders of a global character. Or there is the question of the human itself, urgently needed for a new thought of human rights or bioethics. And it is the task of the humanities to draw these out.

But if there are such questions for the fact of the existence of linguistic events such as literature, this is not to say that they exist as mere topics, problems, or objects of study. For the modality of existence of what calls for thought in this manner does not lend itself immediately to representation and thematization.[47] Where an artistic or linguistic event offers the possibility of rethinking a question such as human experience or a notion such as infancy, it does so in the grain of its articulations, in complex rhetorical modulations or even forms of interruption or stammering. It may take a tonal form, or appear in a certain insistence or even flatness, so that we can say that the language is communicating "im-mediately."[48] The relation it offers to such questions will not surrender to an objectifying conceptual appropriation. Different pragmatics of thought are required, practices of writing, teaching, and creation that bring forth in a searching manner the exigencies proper to them. Research in the humanities, as I am trying to define it, does not conceptualize questions such as community or freedom; rather, it draws them forth as questions, or exigencies, it shows they are there as exigencies as it limns their meaning. Such an endeavor does not abjure the concept, but it always tries to bring the concept back to its limits. It proceeds from the way such questions are given in the "communicability," "legibility," or "translatability" of a text, and in an active form of critique.[49] It will sometimes take on something of a literary character of its own. Or in its conceptual work, it will assume the modality of a "perhaps"—it will suppose its (non)object, seeking to draw forth its own conditions of existence by manifesting its own answerability.[50] Moreover, it may openly assume its engagements and the temporalities proper to them (opening to futurity and/or a sense of being haunted) in a manner like that urged recently by Jacques Derrida. But to the extent that such research is of the humanities, and however modestly it proceeds, it will engage the communicability of its object, and will inevitably show this engagement in its own language.

Again, all of this suggests that "theory"—and I use the term with the caution I noted in my introduction—will not provide a sufficient answer to the question of what is at stake in the humanities. In most of its contemporary instantiations, at least, its very mode of representation cannot but fail, at a certain point, what calls for the humanities. As Jean-François Lyotard would have put it, there is a kind of differend here, and the first task of the humanities, as he understood it, is to testify to that differend. *Sauver l'honneur de penser,* he wrote, risking a phrase that was as

dangerously outmoded then as any stand on behalf of the humanities today.[51] This imperative will only be served by new, creative
forms of critical thinking.

Because the question of the humanities, as Blanchot helps us
understand it, cannot be heard in most theoretical position taking, I believe we must be wary of the temptations offered to the
humanities by the model of the public intellectual. The dilemma
facing the humanities today is not a function of their isolation
within the public sphere; it is rather a function of the representation of the public space itself (which academics, who are tempted
by a kind of journalism, even when they acknowledge the many
constraints on this form of representation, are far too quick to
ratify). And if the Sartrean version of this intellectual role has lost
its credibility by reason of the universalizing pretension it carried
(a point established firmly by Foucault and Jacques Rancière many
years ago), the more recent pragmatic acknowledgment of the
"interested" character of every intervention does little to address
the question of representation itself. I do not mean to suggest here
that intellectuals should eschew public responsibilities and remain
silent on matters of contemporary concern. Not at all. I mean to
insist only that as intellectuals they have the additional burden of
trying to intervene in a manner that contributes to redefining the
very meaning of "public space." Moreover, I think that the task
of defining new ways for understanding the potentially public
character of writing and teaching in the humanities is an urgent
one.[52] But the contemporary understanding of the public intellectual seems inherently to deny the understanding of intellectual
work that assumes the exigencies of local engagement or the kinds
of concerns Michel Foucault and Gilles Deleuze explored when
they advanced their notion of a "local intellectual."[53] One might
even say that it absolves the intellectual of the task of thinking
altogether.

I do not want to return here to Foucault's and Deleuze's dialogue, even if I think there is a great deal that is important in it.
I will simply take over their designation and translate it for the
current discussion by suggesting that the local intellectual working in the fields of the humanities is one who takes the risk of
answering to the exigencies to which I have pointed at each of the

sites at which they present themselves—which is to say in the language or medium of these fields. For a teacher, this means attempting a pedagogy whose ends are quite uncertain in relation to the governing standards of knowledge production and re-production (and working for the local institutional conditions that will allow such pedagogy). It means attending to a set of sin-gular and collective relations by way of a quite concrete medium (be it poetry, film, or philosophy)—not a promotion of world-views or a give-and-take of opinion, but a passage, with others, through a series of questions that open in practices of reading and analysis.[54]

My own specific efforts along these lines in recent years have led me to the question of testimony and historical representa-tion via psychoanalysis, literature, and film. Freud's case studies (risky, open-ended texts that are frequently quite problematic, but also genuinely groundbreaking) have proven to be especially use-ful points of introduction to the question of interpretation and notions such as trauma, the primal scene, and transference. They also allow me to broach questions bearing on the structure and undertaking of this very seminar (issues bearing on pedagogical authority and the temporalities of learning when it is a matter of thinking and not mere assimilation). Blanchot's engagement with psychoanalysis in *The Writing of the Disaster* and related mate-rial in *The Infinite Conversation* has then allowed me to link the problem of representation as it is raised in that discipline with his thought on language and the ethical relation. From there, I have turned to Claude Lanzman's film *Shoah* and have also turned to texts by Primo Levi and Ota Yoko (her astonishing testimonial work *City of Corpses*).[55] At some point in this trajectory (though I cannot say exactly—for essential reasons—when this happens), I convey to students that the questions we are attempting to address have to be read *in the texts* (and in the film), in a very strong sense of this phrase—that they can only really open as *tex-tual events*.[56] It is a point that I repeat in every class from the very first week, but I know that it has to *happen* before it is truly rec-ognized. Testimony from students has convinced me that many do in fact undergo a kind of experience with language (an experi-ence of the limits of representation) in the course of the semester.

This testimony has come most powerfully in the form of creative works submitted for the final project, but also in the evolving character of discussion. Again, I could not pretend to say exactly when and where this experience occurs or what it involves for each student. I do know that my own experience—each time—involves a significant transformation in ethicopolitical awareness and in everyday relations (a richer relation to my everyday experience), and I think I glimpse in some students a similar transformation. What do such transformations prepare? What do they enable in ethical, historical, or even aesthetic understanding? How do they prepare the imaginative capacity of students, their susceptibility to genuine encounter at an interhuman level and in relation to what Jean-François Lyotard called "the event"? These are not questions that admit easy or certain answers. But I am convinced that the experience that occasions such transformations, however fleeting it might be, holds tremendous import for students, for it ultimately involves nothing less than exposure to the grounds of historical and social existence.

The task I am describing remains a local one because it proceeds in and from the material site of the pedagogical relation. It invests in the *relation* (in what can be made to happen there via the medium of study) rather than using the occasion for the rehearsal of timely concepts and themes that are often all too familiar to the students and do little more than challenge opinion (or confirm the good conscience).[57] Strong teaching in the humanities, I believe, always involves an experiential, relational structure like the one to which I have pointed, and thus engages the very grounds of being-together. It certainly need not pass by materials as traumatic as those I have cited, and it involves a great deal of instruction in a very traditional sense, but it also always involves the complex temporalities of an experience with language. In this sense, it touches the limits of any ideological position or worldview and leaves behind all the terms of the culture wars (and thus the boundaries in which the humanities have been contained).

I emphasize pedagogy here because I believe that the flight from the local task of teaching (flight from the very medium of one's teaching practice in the humanities, which is language, and flight from the special forms of obligation that attend engagement in and by this medium in the teaching relation, including respect for the distended, incalculable time of this relation) weighs heavily on the humanities. Or let me say, more precisely, that the difficulty in articulating what is at stake in teaching in the fields of the humanities contributes essentially to the disarray afflicting the self-understanding and self-presentation of their fields. For I see no scorn for the task of teaching. Even graduate assistants who cannot imagine teaching in a primary or secondary school system, for example, are passionately devoted to their assignments. What I see is a lack of clarity about the meaning of teaching in the context of the humanities. Is it possible that this lack of clarity regarding what is at stake in the experience of teaching, particularly in its ethical dimension, has helped create the drift I have described in this area of research, that the lack of an ethicopolitical gravity and bearing in the teaching mission have left research itself rudderless? If faculty could grasp the ethicopolitical dimension of their teaching, would they be so deeply anxious about the political relevance of their work? Would they rush to compensate for the uncertainties faced in the classroom and seminar by politicizing their work (in a shallow fashion) and seeking visibility in the publishing market? The questions seem legitimate, but I believe that the forces of the latter market, fueled as they are by an entire system of academic evaluations and rewards, cannot be underestimated in their impact upon the shape of research itself and the kinds of research introduced into the classroom. Here, the task of the local intellectual is to transform this market by introducing forms of writing that force different temporalities in discussion and reception. If theory, some theory, regains its object—its *pragma*—in such a way that it is *of* the humanities in the way I have tried to suggest in this essay, it will oblige different forms of reading and exchange. For it will shed its instrumental character and will no longer be so easily applicable to those infinite contexts offered by that semblance of an object, "culture," or those vast markets provided by globalization. This is not to say that we can do without analyses of globalization and the hard research pursued in fields such as area studies, but the latter work must be drawn into more local forms of engagement and be made answerable to the claims of human finitude and their immensely complex usages. Appeals to the notion of globalization, for example, must be brought into communication with a thought of "world" or "forms of life."[58] Here, a theory is required that no longer gestures toward difference in general and abstract terms; it must bring forth difference, *speak from difference,* making resonant the fact that *there is* a question of community, a question of freedom, a question of the human in the sites that call for response.

Those who look to theory for its instrumental and representational function for various forms of social transformation will surely be unsatisfied with such a call for more local interventions (interventions, that is, that answer to the sites that call them forth).[59] But I do not think that testifying to the exigencies of community or freedom, and then elaborating their meaning, is a modest task. And I cannot imagine that a consequent thought of what calls for the humanities can be without significance for concerns of a sociopolitical character and even political action. First, it is inevitable that this thought will be won in relation to such concerns (none of us exist outside them). But of equal importance is the fact that such thought *frees* social action, or frees it to its meaning. Not that it confers meaning—philosophy, for example, is not there to provide a ground or ethical answers. Rather, it brings forth the ethical character of every act, and this discovery has a strangely liberating character. It exposes the possibility and necessity of decision, just as it frees initiatives from a debilitating accounting and allows for passage outside boundaries defined by institutions and markets.[60] But even these incalculable results are not the first concern of the humanities, nor is the service articulation from which we started (the role of the humanities in education, civic life, and so on). Their first concern is to make happen the fundamental questions from the basis of which such an articulation becomes imperative. And for those working for the humanities today, the fact of such questions and the exigencies that attend their elaboration must be drawn forth. The articulations will have been happening at every step and will follow inevitably.

Notes

Introduction

1. I will offer what I understand to be a *possible* account of the conditions of fundamental research in the humanities, and a discussion of the kinds of questions that open in a concrete manner from the basis of this approach. With this phrase, "possible account," I mean to make a claim for the founded character of this argument. It seeks to respond, I will suggest, to what language gives of relation. The fact that this offering of relation will be engaged in always singular manners (and only comes about as it is engaged and drawn forth—in an answer that effectively discovers its conditions) prompts me to use the word "possible" and to insist that I am not proposing a foundation. But my account differs from a pragmatic one in that I claim to be engaging the *pragma* of thought. When I write that *there are* humanities, I mean this in a strong sense. One could appropriately call my argument "essentialist," but it rests upon a rethinking of the notion of essence that is inspired by the work of Martin Heidegger, Walter Benjamin, and Maurice Blanchot.

A defense of the humanities for a broad public would focus most appropriately, I believe, on some of the notions I have enumerated as proper to "fundamental research." A broader public should be introduced to what I tried to say about the role of the humanities for any vocation, for example. But the possibility of this research always requires justification, and it is at this level that I pitch my work in this volume.

2. I cite here the title of a brief essay I contributed to the inaugural issue of *Traces* (2001, 231–32). I overstate, to be sure. There have been all kinds of events in the multifold, rapidly transforming domain of theory, and I am fully prepared to acknowledge that I am "doing theory" on many occasions and defend its importance. No doubt, it is advisable to forego general statements about a domain that encompasses these very statements and will not surrender to generalities. I note simply that my few distinctions can be summarized with an opposition between theory and thought. But this is not a clean opposition, and I will use it sparingly. I will place my emphasis, instead, on defining what is meant by the practice of thought.

3. Paul Celan, *Collected Prose*, trans. Rosmarie Waldrop (Riverdale-on-Hudson, NY: Sheep Meadow Press, 1986), 35.

4. I follow Celan in evoking the Heideggerian reference, but this language should be supplemented by the contributions of a wide range of post-Marxist critical work that attends to the modern instrumental rationalities.

5. A sympathetic reader of this book suggested that I could best define the reality at stake for the humanities in the contemporary world by taking up recent discussions of the ideologies informing official American foreign and domestic policy. Whether or not one accepts this political frame as the most pertinent one (I find it a bit too immediate, since the current plight of the humanities quite antedates the contemporary conservative turn), I think it is important to recognize that it implicitly posits that discursive reality is a function of political context and that a greater reality is achieved through a sharpening of the political meaning of a discursive intervention. I do not entirely refuse this assumption, but I believe its truth is limited, and I seek a different sense of the notion of reality in my reflections on the practices of philosophy and on the humanities in general. My argument runs contrary to the widespread contemporary assumption in the academy that "everything is political" (a thoroughly metaphysical proposition). It suggests that discourses in the humanities find real ethicopolitical purchase when they find ways to engage what properly calls for their thinking. Political intervention in the humanities, when it occurs, is conditioned by such engagement and is informed by it. Moreover, interventions that are properly humanistic (and at their most powerful) are interventions in the symbolic—i.e., in that order where political meaning is constituted. There is a major discussion to be pursued here about the political ends of humanistic thought (a topic I take

up, to some extent, in the first section of my first chapter). Here I want to assert simply that one of the aims of the humanities is to think and draw forth the grounds (or nongrounds) of political being and the very possibility of a political relation. Discourses from the humanities almost inevitably take political steps in such thinking (and I firmly believe this necessity is not to be avoided), but if they surrender too quickly to the academic market's demand that they be political, they risk losing what makes them humanistic. I argue that if seeking reality is the end of intellectual engagement in the humanities, it is best pursued by finding ways to engage concretely questions such as the nature of the human (and thus the grounds of the ethicopolitical relation) and the nature and possibilities for human experience amid the managed evidence of the contemporary world.

I therefore offer an ontological account of the limits of the idea that everything is political, but I would also like to applaud recent efforts to contest the politicization of theory by politically engaged authors such as Gayatri Spivak and Wendy Brown.

A Politics of Thought

1. Granel's essay is collected in his *De l'université* (Mauzevin: Trans-Europ-Repress, 1982), 75–96; all translations are my own. The Trans-Europ-Repress was created and directed by Granel himself, and belongs in an important way to the project I will describe (the copyright notice for *De l'université* indicates that it may be reproduced freely in any country except Russia). Its publications were distributed in part by Granel's students. Since most Anglo-American readers will not have heard of Gérard Granel, I should mention that his impressive body of work includes important contributions in the area of phenomenological research: *Le sens du temps et de la perception chez E. Husserl* (Paris: Gallimard, 1969) and *L'équivoque ontologique de la pensée Kantienne* (Paris: Gallimard, 1970), the French translation of Husserl's *Krisis* (*La crise des sciences européennes et la phénoménologie transcendentale* [Paris: Gallimard, 1976]), several stunning collections of essays (*Traditionis Traditio* [Paris: Gallimard, 1972]), *Écrits logiques et politiques* [Paris: Galilée, 1990], and *Études* [Paris: Galilée, 1995]), and a professorial career whose importance is attested to in the recent commemorative volume edited by Jean-Luc Nancy and Élisabeth Rigal, *Granel, l'éclat, le combat, l'ouvert* (Paris: Bélin, 2001). A review of this last volume in *Le Monde* expresses astonishment at the strength of testimony from distinguished scholars regarding this relatively obscure figure. To account for his obscurity, I can only note that he was a proud and uncompromising

thinker who remained on the margins of the Parisian theater; he was a difficult individual, but one of the most highly regarded teachers I have had the pleasure of encountering.

2. Published in the *Graduate Faculty Philosophy Journal of the New School for Social Research* 14, no. 2/15, no. 1 (1991): 335–62.

3. Bill Readings, *The University in Ruins* (Cambridge: Harvard University Press, 1996). I had the pleasure of entering into a dialogue with Readings on this topic before his death, but missed the opportunity to respond to a footnote in the volume in which he noted his proximity to my arguments in my original essay on Granel and his hesitations regarding something he termed my "optimism." Readings noted that I was holding (after Heidegger and with Granel) to a faith in the idea of the university. He did not avoid an invocation of Heidegger of his own in the final chapters of his book (I refer to his important reference to the Heideggerian notion of thought), but he saw that I had repeated Heidegger's questionable assumption that the university could play a fundamental role in social transformation. I would have to say that the autocritique I have pursued in this new version of my essay actually derives from numerous sources, but I want to acknowledge that I have come to accept Readings's implicit criticism. I also hope that I am able to develop his reference to a "thought" that should guide any future "dwelling" in the ruins of the university (here, and in "The Claim of Language: A Case for the Humanities").

4. *Traditionis Traditio,* 103.

5. Jacques Derrida, *Of Grammatology,* trans. Gayatri Spivak (Baltimore: Johns Hopkins University Press, 1976), 46.

6. Ibid., 24. Derrida would not repeat such a statement today, but I emphasize that he has not hesitated to argue for a fundamental turn for thought in the university. This is the topic of "Acts of Engagement" in the present volume.

7. This would be a deconstructive version, in other words, of something Heidegger described in paragraph 3 of *Being and Time* as the pursuit of a "productive logic" (*Being and Time,* trans. John Macquarrie and Edward Robinson [New York: Harper and Row, 1962], 29–31).

8. "Et Tu, Quis Es?," *Critique* 39, no. 369 (1978): 179.

9. *Traditionis Traditio,* 106–7; emphasis in original.

10. Let me try to recall this briefly. Thought, as Derrida refers to his practice in *Of Grammatology,* moves from a generalization of a concept taken from a positive science (the concept of the arbitrariness of the sign) to the notion of the "instituted trace" it presupposes. The latter, what Derrida calls "writing," can only be pursued in a form of transcendental

reflection because it describes not only the condition of possibility of any linguistic system, but the condition of any objectivity and any experience in general. As Derrida puts it, "What thus seems to be produced within an ontic field or within a regional ontology [the concept of the instituted trace] does not belong to them by rights and already leads back to the question of Being itself" (22). But Derrida then subjects the presuppositions of transcendental reflection to a thought of writing and demonstrates that the thought of the trace cannot function in isolation from empirical research. "Grammatology" thus names a constantly renewed *passage* between positive science and transcendental reflection that is irreducible to either of them—"the *necessary* path for thought today": "It is no doubt necessary to undertake a reflection in which 'positive' discovery, and the 'deconstruction' of the history of metaphysics in all its concepts, control one another reciprocally, minutely, laboriously" (83). And this for the sake of what Derrida named in an interview from that period "a more powerful and transforming science" ("Ja, ou le faux-bond," *Digraphe* 11 [April 1977]: 104).

11. Granel will sometimes speak of "le tout" (the whole), and occasionally of "totality," invoking with this last term both the totality of what is *(das Seiendes),* and the totality in the sense of the world, as defined by Heidegger (thus he can speak of the totality of knowledge provided by the sciences without, inasmuch, denying the existence of another knowledge—the knowledge, as he puts it, of "death, play, risk, and practice" [*Traditionis Traditio,* 13]: a knowledge deriving from the experience of finite transcendence that discloses to the Dasein its world). But Granel will normally use "the whole" to refer to the Dasein's world. Consider, for example, these words on the nature of his political objective in the context of a present to which the dual reign of capital and *Technik* (Heidegger's term for the era of technicity) has denied any "historical" future: "There is nothing to be 'done' against an age of Being. But there is a lot to prepare. . . . And we concede that this 'lot' is destined to remain nothing if it does not become everything *(tout),* but this will also be (and even first of all) in taking our distance from the idea of totality. 'Political power'—both the first condition of all serious action until now and the inaccessible end of an interminable militancy—like the 'global discourse' to which every organization feels obliged and of which it finds itself incapable, are henceforth no longer objects for us" (*De l'université,* 65). I will return to this citation later, but I might note in anticipation that my concluding questions will focus in part on the meaning of Granel's problematic phrase, "this 'lot' is destined to remain nothing if it does not become everything."

12. *Traditionis Traditio,* 13.

13. I am drawing here upon Jean-Luc Nancy's notion of a *partage,* developed in *Le partage des voix* (Paris: Galilée, 1982). *Partager* means both to share and to divide.

14. *De l'université,* 93.

15. Ibid., 65.

16. The remarks on Nietzsche in "Preliminaries for Something Else, I" point in this direction (*De l'université,* 55–56), and later remarks in relation to Heidegger (121) are quite explicit in this regard.

17. I develop this argument at some length in the original version of this paper, "But Suppose We Were to Take the Rectorial Address Seriously."

18. I should emphasize that this question of the subject of the praxis of existence (Granel's effort to grasp for whom and by whom the fundamental critique he envisions might be undertaken) preoccupies him deeply. In the original version of this paper (ibid.), I try to outline the temptation he documents of appealing to some notion of "the popular"; it is visible in the tone with which he refuses any genealogy (including an interesting one he sketches via the surrealists, Benjamin, Brecht, Gramsci, and Eisenstein) that would allow one to invoke this latter notion. Ultimately, Granel does not allow us to ask for whom his project might be undertaken—he will not give a figure to the exposure of the historicity and materiality of existence he envisions.

19. *De l'université,* 92.

20. Though one still has to ask why Granel appeals to that rhetoric. It is true that he draws constantly from rhetorical forms whose presuppositions he also criticizes, and there is no doubt that the one he adopts here had considerably more force when he wrote his essay that it does today (it was the still quite viable language of the French *extrême gauche*). But there is a rather heavy price to be paid for such rhetorical indulgence, as Granel surely saw in the case of Heidegger (whose rhetorical compromises were utterly condemnable). I suspect that Jean-François Lyotard's violent reaction to Granel in *Heidegger and the Jews* (trans. Andreas Michel and Mark Roberts [Minneapolis: University of Minnesota Press, 1990]) is in large measure attributable to Lyotard's allergy to Granel's rhetorical excesses, and particularly the rhetoric of sovereignty. Of course, if Granel is indulging in a political reverie here, I must state clearly that this strategy strikes me (has always struck me) as utterly regressive, even reactionary. A great deal rests here upon what Granel means by the phrase "from outside."

21. "We are not inviting people to leave the public sphere in order to enter into philosophy, rather we are calling for an overturning of the

forms of knowledge in their ideologico-institutional reality, as the premise and lever for an overturning of the entire current reality. This is something other than continuing the production of our individual texts, each of us on our own, even if they should happen to produce effects of slippage, displacement, or even rupture for the audience of 'minds'" (*De l'université*, 94).

22. Many have sketched the avatars of that ambition, and I won't pause to retrace its history from its Kantian articulation through what Readings calls "the university of culture." It is a notion of the academy, I would add, that allows a considerable number of intellectuals in the humanities and social sciences to imagine that their critical endeavors have direct cultural significance, that despite the extensive mediations of the institutional structures in which they are embedded, their work shapes social understanding immediately—an assumption to which there is almost inevitably coupled the idea that true intellectual activity exists only in the university, that thought has no real life outside it.

23. Granel's rhetoric is always breathtaking, and it is particularly so here. He argues that the university has represented historically "a kind of poetico-politico-philosophical whirlwind in which the historical existence of the various peoples works at its self-knowledge: says itself, thinks itself, and wills itself" (*De l'université*, 78). His elaboration of the meaning of his phrase can be traced directly to Heidegger. Within the defining limits of this founding idea, Granel argues, the university has served two functions: a free development of the various forms of knowledge, and a preparation of an elite for various professions and positions of leadership. Granel seeks to release the first of these functions by proposing that the university should cease to prepare individuals for a social function and should devote itself to the freedom that presides in the pragmatics of knowledge.

24. And with regard to my dear friend William Spanos, I can say it has been a point of productive controversy for many years. I cite his work here only because I have the highest respect for his intelligence, intellectual integrity, and dedication.

25. I am thinking, here, more of recent movements to think globalization (and empire) than of Granel himself. But I am also suspicious of his reference to "the triply rational language of economy, politics, and technique." Can the many forms of practice in these domains be gathered in a single logic? Of course, this suspicion goes to the heart of the project I described at the outset of this essay. My struggle with Granel's political translation of that project is in large measure a struggle with the guiding assumption that a philosophical thought embracing the totality

of knowledge is possible. It would appear to me now that a thought of practical finitude irrevocably disrupts such an assumption. Derrida would appear to acknowledge this point in his own project for the Collège International de Philosophie (and thus take a distance from some of the statements from the time of *Of Grammatology* I cited earlier). Assuming a thought of practical finitude, I would argue, requires a thorough elaboration of the notions of singularity and multiplicity. And as I have emphasized throughout these pages, it requires a new thought of the relationality of the always multiplying forms of practice.

26. Political action, I should emphasize, is another matter. Where it is a question of addressing injustice and violence (of all kinds), a practice of representation is essential. The injustice must be named and rectified. I do not want to deny in any way that there is a very important place in the academy for this kind of work. What I am attempting to address here, with Granel, is an ethicopolitical practice where the stakes are "existence in a world." I would argue that political action, while essential, must at some point address these more fundamental stakes if it is to bring forth the always open meaning of terms like "justice," "freedom," or "the human." The latter task belongs to thought. With Jean-Luc Nancy and Philippe Lacoue-Labarthe, I once tried to work at a distinction between "politics" and "the political" (where the grounds of the political relation are in play). The distinction seems unavoidable in some respects, but I have found that it is often bridged in local forms of political negotiation (particularly where peace must be negotiated).

27. This is what Walter Benjamin understood in his effort to develop a notion of critique adequate to the "weak" messianic power of the past.

28. Hölderlin defined a still urgent task for modernity, I believe, when he attempted to think the possibility of assuming time (reversing the "flight" that characterized German Idealism—a tendency in modernity that he linked to Greek "enthusiasm" in his chiasmic construction of the relation between the ancients and the moderns). My effort to understand what it might mean to affirm finitude and my wariness regarding a universalizing or globalizing temptation could well be developed in these terms.

29. Candace D. Lang develops this distinction between irony and humor in *Irony/Humor: Critical Paradigms* (Baltimore: Johns Hopkins University Press, 1988). One of her principal guides in this study, I believe, is Jean-François Lyotard, and I follow her in this respect. For another important articulation of this notion, see Gilles Deleuze and Claire Parnet, *Dialogues,* trans. Hugh Tomlinson and Barbara Habberjam (New York: Columbia University Press, 1987), 68–69. One might also consult

Jacques Lacan's remarkable statement in the opening pages of the *The Four Fundamental Concepts of Psychoanalysis,* trans. Alan Sheridan (New York: W. W. Norton, 1981), 4–5. I suspect that such a notion of humor can be developed from Heidegger's notion of the recognition of inauthenticity that occurs in *Ereignis,* but I will have to demonstrate this on another occasion.

30. Maurice Blanchot, *The Infinite Conversation,* trans. Susan Hanson (Minneapolis: University of Minnesota Press, 1993), 192. I am prompted to cite here, as a kind of allegory of what I am seeking, a famous tale regarding Rabbi Shimeon ben Yohai, who was forced to go into hiding with his son after some rather uncompromising words concerning the Roman occupying forces. Emerging at the behest of Elijah the prophet after twelve years of study and prayer in a cave, Rabbi Shimeon and his son are confronted with the aspect of everyday life pursuing its course and burn everything they see in rage at this neglect of eternal life. A voice from heaven intervenes to ask, "Would you destroy my world?" and then commands them to return to their cave for a year (for punishment in hell lasts no more than twelve months). At their reemergence, they encounter an old man with two bunches of myrtle in his hands in honor of the *Shabbath*. Attaining at this moment a new understanding of the gift of the divine *mitzvot,* they are reconciled with the world. In short, Granel's error reminds me of Rabbi Shimeon's. I cite this story without intending any reference to the contemporary situation in the Middle East, but I would note that a thought of peace is inherent in it, and I hope to pursue this thought in coming work.

Acts of Engagement

1. These writings are collected in *Du droit à la philosophie* (Paris: Galilée, 1990) and range from the earliest essays written for GREPH (the Groupe de Recherches sur l'Enseignement de la Philosophie—an initiative to which I devoted an essay some years ago: "A Deceleration of Philosophy," *Diacritics* 8, no. 2 [Summer 1978]: 80–90)—to the more recent efforts on behalf of the Collège International de Philosophie. Derrida has recently added to this work a short volume entitled *L'université sans condition* (Paris: Galilée, 2001); though I will not consider it here, it contains a relevant discussion of the topic of engagement in relation to a notion of professing.

2. "Sendoffs," trans. Thomas Pepper, in *Reading the Archive: On Texts and Institutions,* ed. E. S. Burt and Janie Vanpée, Yale French Studies, no. 77 (New Haven, CT: Yale University Press, 1990), 7–43.

3. Derrida does not evoke the contemporary concept of globalization

(a concept he would undoubtedly want to question) in this essay of 1982, but his enumeration of issues clearly indicates his attention to this new challenge to the articulation of philosophy's topoi.

4. *Du droit à la philosophie,* 560; translation my own.

5. Ibid., 20. Derrida is working here through the imperatives of a thought of "finite transcendence." While the act of thought is not reducible to the determinations of its sociopolitical or linguistic context, it cannot be abstracted from its finite, always historical, inscription.

6. Ibid., 35.

7. *Specters of Marx,* trans. Peggy Kamuf (New York: Routledge, 1994), 31.

8. "The thought of this 'yes' *before* philosophy, *before* even the question, *before* research and critique, does not signify any renunciation of philosophy, or of what might follow it or follow from it. This thought *can,* and one might even think that precisely it *must,* engage itself there. It can do so inasmuch as, under the form of obligation or debt, it finds itself already *engaged,* already inscribed in the space that is opened and closed by this *gage*—given to the other, received from the other. But it traces a kind of strange limit between all these determinations of the philosophical and a deconstructive thought that is engaged *by* philosophy without belonging to it, faithful to an affirmation whose responsibility places it *before* philosophy, but also *in advance* of it" (*Du droit à la philosophie,* 28; emphasis in original).

9. Ibid., 561.

10. Ibid., 587.

11. Derrida gives the following summary description of the reach of this motif: "Let's not unfold this problematic in its most easily identifiable dimensions yet (destination and destiny, all the problems of the end and thus of limits or of confines, ethical or political aim, teleology—natural or not—, the destination of life, of man, of history, the problem of eschatology (utopian, religious, revolutionary, etc.), that of the constitution and the structure of the sender/receiver system, and thus of the dispatch or sendoff and the message (in all its forms and in all its substances— linguistic or not, semiotic or not), emission, the mission, the missile, transmission in all its forms, telecommunication and all its techniques, economic distribution and all its conditions (producing, giving, receiving, exchanging), the dispensation of knowledge and what we now call the ['finalisation'] of research or of techno-science, etc.)" ("Sendoffs," 14).

12. *Du droit à la philosophie,* 29.

13. Ibid., 592.

14. *Specters of Marx*, 74–75.

15. A regrettable limitation, perhaps, since it clearly points to a further-reaching thought of the event than the one subsequently offered by Alain Badiou (whose understanding of the question of language remains far short of what would be required by a consequent thought of performativity in the sense sought by Derrida). See Badiou's *Manifeste pour la philosophie* (Paris: Editions du Seuil, 1989).

16. *Specters of Marx*, 22–23.

17. This phrase ("*the* relation") does not appear in the English translation of *On the Way to Language*. See Martin Heidegger, *Unterwegs zur Sprache, Gesamtausgabe* (Frankfurt am Main: Klostermann, 1985), 12: 229. The German reads, "*das* Ver-Hältnis."

18. *Specters of Marx*, 26.

19. Derrida consistently leaves untouched the problematic of usage at the ontological level, and nothing in his argument will help us determine whether he is avoiding the topic, unaware of it, or simply uninterested. It seems quite possible to me that he declines engagement with it in Heidegger's text because it would oblige him to take up the issue of Heidegger's references to a "human essence" that is appropriated to language in *Ereignis*, a reference to the human that functions at a level quite different from the one at which he pursued his critique of Heidegger's "humanism." In any case, Derrida's strong resistance to any appeal to the philosopheme of *l'homme*, however "deconstructed," could well explain a reluctance to work with the term. At the same time, however, it is possible to find traces in his text of a thought of usage like the one I am attempting to explore. In *Force de loi* (Paris: Galilée, 1994), for example, Derrida evokes a "heteronomy" in the "mad" act of decision (one that answers to the urgency of every just decision): "Such a decision is at once super-active *and* suffered, it retains something passive about it, even unconscious, as though the decider were free only to let themselves be affected by their own decision, and as though the latter came to them from the other. The consequences of such a heteronomy are forbidding, but it would be unjust to avoid the necessity." (This sentence appears only in the French edition of Derrida's essay; for the English, see "Force of Law: The Mystical Foundation of Authority," trans. Mary Quaintance, in *Cardozo Law Review* 11, no. 5/6 [1990]: 919–1046). I would also note that Derrida's attention to the materiality of the human Dasein as it is described in *Being and Time* engages the topic of the bodily character of what Heidegger declares to be the "proper" of the human essence that is appropriated by language (though Derrida does not take it up in

these terms and does not discuss this later notion of the "appropriation" of the human to language in *Ereignis*). See the two essays under the title "Geschlecht" in *Psyché: Inventions de l'autre* (Paris: Galilée, 1987), 395–452. Do we still "accompany" Derrida by pursuing a path like this one? This might be the point to observe that I have always considered accompaniment to mean working with Derrida, not on him or simply after him. To write on Derrida or to repeat his thought in a doctrinal manner is perhaps the best way to neutralize the deconstructive force of his engagements.

20. *Unterwegs zur Sprache*, 250.

21. Heidegger describes this powerlessness in his essay "Gelassenheit" as follows: "The essence of humankind is released into that which regions and accordingly used by it for this reason alone: because humankind for itself has no power over truth and the latter remains independent of it" (*Discourse on Thinking*, trans. John M. Anderson and E. Hans Freund [New York: Harper and Row, 1966], 84). I have attempted to work through the implications of this passage in *Language and Relation: . . . That There Is Language* (Stanford, CA: Stanford University Press, 1996) in the course of a lengthy reading of Heidegger's *On the Way to Language*. While I cannot reproduce this analysis here, I would note that it points to the necessity of thinking a fundamental interruption in the relation between Being and humankind. Pushing Heidegger's analysis in this way (which is to say, reading the trace of this interruption in his text), we come into proximity with Derrida's thought of the experience of justice. It is on this basis that I feel it is worthwhile to develop the "schema" of destination in relation to a notion of usage.

22. It would be useful, for our purposes, to review the "quasi-transcendental" status of this "yes" that resembles, as Derrida puts it, "an absolute performative." A careful examination of the manner in which Derrida removes it both from the hold of any linguistic science and from any ontological or transcendental discourse would demonstrate just how great a challenge his thought of destination pursued in relation to a notion of usage poses to any traditional understanding of the role of philosophy or its relation to other discourses and practices. Here, for example, are the concluding words of his summary ("naïve") statement on the status of any discourse addressed to this condition of all discourse ("Nombre de oui," in *Psyché*, 649): "And yet, *one must*—yes—maintain the ontologico-transcendental requirement in order to bring forth the dimension of a *yes* that is no more empirical or ontical than it is subject to any science, ontology, regional phenomenology, or finally any predicative discourse. Presupposed by every proposition, it cannot be confused

with the position, thesis, or theme of any language. It is through and through that fable which, inasmuch as it is 'quasi' before the act and before the *logos,* remains 'quasi' at the beginning: 'With the word *with* this text thus begins . . .' [Par le mot *par* commence donc ce texte . . .] (Ponge, 'Fable')." But to do any justice to the honor paid to Michel de Certeau's memory in this essay, it would be equally necessary to attend to the "quasi-analytic" account of the necessity of repetition to which I have referred: an extraordinary rendition of the "promise of memory and [the] memory of the promise" (*Psyché,* 649). Here, Derrida carries forward Heidegger's thought of the multifold character of the engagement with language I have described in an extremely free and compelling manner. (One should also consult the analysis of the promise in Derrida's *Mémoires*—another text that engages at some length Heidegger's meditations on the *Zusage* of language.) Thus, I must reiterate that while Derrida works through the structure of this "originary performative" in a way that is quite consistent with Heidegger (explicitly consistent at some points—constant reference is made to Heidegger's thought of language's address and an anticipatory response), his description of the divided, repetitive character of its "enunciation" clearly departs from the Heideggerian account (which accords its own place to a notion of repetition). Any thought of a Derridean *Sprachgebrauch* would have to take account of this thought of a divided enunciation.

23. If "ontological" is understood in reference to "the discourse on the being of a presence" ("Nombre de oui," 648), as it almost always is, then it proves unsuitable here. I use it only to indicate a level of discourse that engages a thought of Being in its relationality. "Existential," in its turn, remains burdened by the metaphysics of subjectivity, though it seems to me that Jean-Luc Nancy has done quite a bit to free the term "existence" from that legacy.

24. For Derrida's appeal to a notion of experience, see, for example, *Specters of Marx*: "a certain experience of the messianic experience" (59), "the experience of the impossible" (65), "We prefer to say *messianic* rather than *messianism,* so as to designate a structure of experience rather than a religion" (167). In *Force de loi,* Derrida follows Heidegger in thinking the notion of experience from a notion of passage or traversal (see Heidegger's remarks on experience in *On the Way to Language* [New York: Harper and Row, 1971], 57) and evokes a paradoxical "experience of the aporia": "Experience finds its way, its passage, it is possible. In this sense, there cannot be a full experience of the aporia, namely of what does not allow passage. *Aporía* is a non-path. Justice would be, from this point of view, the experience of that which we cannot experience. . . .

But I believe that there is no justice without this experience, however impossible it may be, of the aporia. Justice is an experience of the impossible. A will, a desire, a demand for justice whose structure was not an experience of aporia would have no chance of being what it is, namely a just *call* for justice" (*Force de loi,* 38).

25. "The mystical foundation of authority" is a phrase Derrida takes from Montaigne and Pascal to think the performative (and abyssal) character of any institution of law. Pascal's formulation of the notion reads as follows: "Custom is the sole basis for equity, for the simple reason that it is received; this is the *mystical foundation* of its *authority*" (cited in "Force of Law," 939; my emphasis). Taking a freedom similar to the one Derrida claims in his interpretation of the phrase, I cannot help but suggest that a notion of usage (which inevitably evokes a notion of mores or custom) will help us think the "silence walled up in the violence of the founding act" ("Force of Law," 943). Derrida's own reference to Wittgenstein in this context (to define his understanding of the term "mystical") prompts me to invoke another, namely, Wittgenstein's argument that "meaning is usage." But while Wittgenstein's text actually lends itself in some ways to a thought of the "mystical" along the lines I seek to suggest (a thought of disruptive relation between "Being" and "human being"), it remains quite recalcitrant.

26. See *Psyché,* 644. I draw this phrase, "silent companion," from the passage by Franz Rosenzweig cited by Derrida.

27. Not to speak of the distinctive cast of his writing—rhetorical performative gestures that bear the mark of a singular signature. It is important to recall that the "acts of engagement" I am considering here cannot be thought apart from their occasion and their individual articulation. The "yes" occurs only as it is "drawn out" or "written out," only in its repetition. The same point must be recalled in reference to the notion of accompaniment, with which I will conclude.

28. *Specters of Marx,* 27; emphasis in original.

29. Ibid., 67.

30. Ibid., 21.

31. Derrida evokes this Benjaminian notion in *Specters of Marx,* 96.

The Claim of Language

1. Let me note that I refer here to a context larger than that of my own university. At Binghamton, I have indeed encountered the phenomenon I describe (an assistant to the vice president for research declared irritably, not long ago, that the humanities had to find a way to be "relevant"—a stunning word in the current political context). But I have also

encountered significant interest. The striking thing about these expressions of interest is that they seem so *surprised*. It is as though a broad-gauged initiative on behalf of the humanities (beyond the usual departmental scrambling) is quite unexpected. Let me add that this essay would probably not have been undertaken were it not for a surprised and very affirmative challenge from my university provost, Mary Ann Swain.

2. General, but not universal, and probably shrinking. Recent debates over censorship indicate how fragile this consensus actually is.

3. *The Humanities in American Life* (Berkeley: University of California Press, 1980).

4. Indeed, one cannot even presuppose that "the humanities" are founded on some notion of humanism. Accordingly, I will risk some rhetorical awkwardness by not referring to those who work in the disciplines of the humanities as "humanists." In the latter part of this essay, I will try to define how the humanities can proceed from a new thought of the human, but I will not propose a new "humanism" by reason of the inertia in this term. I do not believe one can escape the historical weight of such a word very easily. A term such as "the human," on the other hand, retains a certain indefiniteness.

5. "The essence of the humanities is a spirit or an attitude toward humanity. They show how the individual is autonomous and at the same time bound, in the ligatures of language and history, to humankind across time and throughout the world" (*The Humanities in American Life,* 3).

6. Numerous references might be appropriate here, but let me cite one that I have found particularly thought provoking for an analysis of the socioeconomic factors determining the possibilities for political agency in the contemporary world (and thus many of the positions occupied in the culture wars). Wendy Brown's analyses in *States of Injury* (Princeton, NJ: Princeton University Press, 1995) and *Politics out of History* (Princeton, NJ: Princeton University Press, 2001) carry the breadth and force necessary for an effort to confront a range of global political realities that threaten to overwhelm the thinker or the activist.

7. Whereas a casual reader of its treatment of theoretical models with antihumanist implications might conclude that the *Times* showed a consistently conservative bias (and even some irresponsibility in its manner of trivializing theoretical positions), the larger agenda was not entirely ideological. By ridiculing the tenor of theoretical debate in the academy, the *Times* gradually worked to arrogate for itself a new critical purchase over academic research. There was a defense of traditional humanism here, and a play for the political and cultural power that is inseparable from such symbolic authority. A related point regarding a displacement

in cultural authority, and perhaps a very important one, can be made in relation to the challenge to secular humanism mounted by the "religious right" and represented in Congress (and now the White House) by the Republican Party. The implications of this challenge for the role of the humanities in education and for their place in the public sphere cannot be underestimated.

8. The situation varies from institution to institution, and crucial differences must be recognized between the missions of public universities and their private counterparts. The latter inevitably serve interests that require some attention to the idea of culture. But are the forces driving public institutions so far from overtaking what is now becoming a kind of final preserve for advanced research in the humanities?

9. Michael Hardt and Antonio Negri, *Empire* (Cambridge: Harvard University Press, 2000). See *New York Times,* July 7, 2001. I hope the reader will allow me these references to a paper I love to hate; it is difficult to avoid them since I face my frustrations with the newspaper's cultural politics at almost every breakfast.

10. See J. Hillis Miller's *Black Holes* (Stanford, CA: Stanford University Press, 1999) for a significant discussion of this point.

11. I return here to a point noted in my essay on Derrida's work ("Acts of Engagement") on the institution of philosophy. I agree with Derrida's argument that a research project requires an engagement that defines what such a project is to *be* (defining its sense in an ontological and existential manner). This is not to deny sociohistorical determinations; rather, it is to affirm the *fundamental* cast of thought in its specific historical site.

12. Of course, one must acknowledge what types of work one has in mind here. The Cornell authors are undoubtedly pointing to sophisticated, theoretically informed work in the social sciences, whereas my citation of the phrase also points back to more unreflective, empirical forms of inquiry. Nevertheless, I believe that there is a real question of limits here that must be broached in a consequent manner. Needless to say, the social sciences cannot be characterized in a blanket fashion; a considerable amount of work in the respective fields is philosophically advanced and quite challenging. The real question facing the humanities and social sciences is: how can we think the relations between these forms of practice and envision productive and transformative passages? In "Acts of Engagement" I suggest that a new thought of the humanities would point to their potential implication in disciplines throughout the fields of knowledge, and indicate how they are needed. As I turn briefly to Foucault below, I will suggest one way in which this relation might be

thought. I hope to pursue the larger project (concerning modes of knowing) on another occasion.

13. Gayatri Chakravorty Spivak, *Death of a Discipline* (New York: Columbia University Press, 2003). This volume came to my notice in the final stages of my preparation of this manuscript and proved immensely heartening since it seems to contain conclusions very similar to ones advanced here (and even in the conclusion of my essay on Granel, "A Politics of Thought"). The heartening factor comes from the fact that the agreement was produced along two very different paths of reflection and practice.

14. At Binghamton University, a recent initiative on behalf of the humanities quickly revealed that it was impossible to speak for the humanities without drawing from a number of voices in the social sciences. I thank my colleague Dale Tomich, from the Sociology Department, for helping me understand some of the dimensions of these shared concerns.

15. An understanding of literature like this one is reflected in Peggy Kamuf's *The Division of Literature, or The University in Deconstruction* (Chicago: University of Chicago Press, 1997).

16. My colleague William Haver has argued this point for many years and has helped bring home to me its importance. I am pleased to find an equally strong and uncompromising advocacy of language study in Spivak's *The Death of a Discipline*. Spivak (another alumnus of Cornell) places the imperative of language study at the heart of her vision of a new comparative literature and links it to the virtues of training in close literary study. I strongly support her argument, particularly when she asserts that literary study can prepare the imagination for what she calls "othering" (and adds that the benefits of such study can be dramatically shaped by experience in the classroom). In the latter part of this essay, I will attempt to give an account of language that might help justify this assertion.

17. I develop this point in *The International Encyclopedia for the Social and Behavioral Sciences* (London: Elsevier, 2001), and present there the reading of Foucault to which I will turn shortly.

18. I would add that the evasion of the "fundamental" dimensions of the linguistic turn is particularly dramatic in modern American pragmatism, which is far more casual than its mentor, Ludwig Wittgenstein, was in facing the question of language as an ontological and ethical question. I address this evasion in the work of Richard Rorty in "Community and the Limits of Theory," in *Community at Loose Ends,* ed. Miami Theory Collective (Minneapolis: University of Minnesota Press, 1987), 19–29.

19. Michel Foucault, "The Discourse on Language," in *The Archaeology of Knowledge and the Discourse on Language*, trans. A. M. Sheridan Smith (New York: Pantheon, 1972), 228–29.

20. Ibid., 227. For a slightly different but highly nuanced version of Foucault's point, one might consider a volume such as Lawrence Venuti's *The Scandals of Translation: Towards an Ethics of Difference* (New York: Routledge, 1998). The resistances to which Foucault points are richly documented in a range of areas pertaining to translation, from "authorship" and "copyright" to "the formation of cultural identities" and "globalization"—all chapter titles. Venuti points to a material "remainder" in language deriving from irreducible differences between languages and from forms of difference at work in each language that escape efforts at control. His emphasis on the politics of idiomatic difference makes his understanding of this remainder diverge somewhat from the one I advance in this essay, which is more ontological and ethical (in a Levinasian sense). But I admire his important work in this area and share his critical aims.

21. We have reached a point, I'm told, where a prominent historian at Binghamton felt able to declare with satisfaction recently that "the linguistic turn is out of fashion"!

22. I emphasize in part because this is the point where my essay diverges from most deconstructive thought in North America.

23. Jacques Lacan, "The Function and Field of Speech and Language in Psychoanalysis," in *Écrits: A Selection*, trans. Alan Sheridan (New York: W. W. Norton, 1977), 30–112.

24. I would note, however, that Lacan's text is badly in need of recovery along lines I wish to sketch in this essay—and I refer not only to the "Function and Field" essay. In psychoanalytic studies today, one witnesses an appeal to a clinical perspective that almost inevitably results in an evisceration of Lacan's text. The effort to clarify Lacan's theory and render it manipulatable in a clinical context has all but stripped the text of its most fundamental dimensions (dimensions to which Lacan appealed repeatedly and explicitly—as, for example, in the seminar *The Four Fundamental Concepts of Metaphysics* or the important essay "The Agency of the Letter"). Lacan's ongoing effort to found psychoanalysis carried him into one of the most profound engagements with modern philosophy available in twentieth-century thought. At the same time, he made it quite clear that his teaching was inseparable from the acts of writing that he performed. Literary theorists, at least, should be capable of reading this text in its performative and poietic dimensions. And perhaps it is not altogether unreasonable to expect some attention to the language of a text (or a dream) from practicing psychoanalysts.

25. I discuss this point in the opening section of *Language and Relation* in the course of a brief discussion of Wittgenstein's "Lecture on Ethics." In the pages that follow, I will occasionally draw upon the textual analyses of this volume for assertions that I cannot pause to justify fully in this essay.

26. I would add that these remarks on the historical precedents of contemporary thought on language should be brought to bear on every aspect of the "fundamental research" whose possibility I am exploring. Whatever research in the humanities is to become, it must have a profound historical component; it must engage the history of thought and practice as it attempts to write the present. But history writing (or any writing of the present—a phrase I draw implicitly from Walter Benjamin) remains in itself a remarkably neglected area in contemporary thinking. Is this another indication of the state of the humanities?

27. *The Archaeology of Knowledge*, 27.

28. In isolating Foucault's description of the *énoncé*, I am slipping into the eye of a kind of theoretical storm and ducking the unrelenting winds of abstraction that Foucault directs at the anthropocentric edifice of the history of ideas. I will leave to others (to the social scientists, first of all) the task of judging the extent to which these theoretical formulations do indeed become—or can become—concrete in historical practice, and will suppose only that if his description of the elementary character of a discursive event is itself concrete, then the archaeology he pursues is itself possible. As for Foucault's detachment of the statement from formal analysis, Foucault argues that the existence of a statement does not require the presence of a propositional structure, and that two statements that are indistinguishable from a logical perspective can function very differently in their respective discursive situations. A statement does not need to take the structure of a sentence; classificatory tables or graphs, algebraic formulas or distribution clouds all entail rules of usage and laws of construction but do not yield to the critique of grammaticality applicable to a natural language. The notion of the speech act captures the event character of a discursive statement, but there are more statements than there are speech acts.

29. *The Archaeology of Knowledge*, 89.

30. Ibid., 109. It is not hidden, Foucault emphasizes, because it defines "the modalities of existence proper to a group of effectively produced signs." Foucault resolutely refuses any allegorical impetus that tracks an unsaid or an unspoken in what is said; the statement's truth does not lie anywhere behind it—either as a distant origin, a hidden meaning, or as a haunting trace that would hollow it out from within. On the other

hand, Foucault says, the statement is not quite visible because of its very transparency. Like the presentation Jean-François Lyotard assigns to the universe of a phrase (see the long discussion of this notion in *The Differend*, trans. Georges Van Den Abbeele [Minneapolis: University of Minnesota Press, 1988], 59–85), the statement's presence does not normally appear except as the referent of another statement.

31. *The Archaeology of Knowledge*, 111.

32. Ibid.

33. Ibid., 113.

34. A similar configuration may be observed in the work of Jean-François Lyotard, who explicitly refused the Heideggerian reference to a "need" for the human on the part of language (thereby acknowledging the passage through the "straits" Foucault defined in *The Order of Things* between the being of language and the being of man), and then turned to a notion of infancy in his latest work to account for a bodily receptivity to the event. Such a notion of "affectability" was certainly present in *The Differend;* but the importance it assumed under the name of "infancy" for Lyotard's later understanding of the very possibility of an event is such as to oblige us to rethink his earlier pragmatics.

35. I touch here on an immense problem concerning the definition of the human in its relation to animals, particularly as it concerns the question of language. Jacques Derrida has pressed this question most firmly in a series of essays that will undoubtedly soon take book form. I do not believe, however, that Derrida's arguments challenge the statement I have made here. A deconstruction of the border between the animal and the human does not do away with the problem of thinking the conditions of human speech (or, for that matter, those of the forms of speech of animals). I take the question of the relation between the human and animals to be of very great importance, but I believe that to the extent we attempt to think the ethical and ontological dimensions of language, we must raise the question of the human (if only to rethink the difference between the human and animals in entirely new ways).

36. These points are made in Heidegger's essays "The Nature of Language" and "The Way to Language," in *On the Way to Language*, trans. Peter D. Hertz (New York: Harper and Row, 1974).

37. The richest account of an answering performative that I know comes in Emmanuel Levinas's "The Temptation of Temptation," in *Nine Talmudic Readings*, trans. Annette Aronowicz (Bloomington: Indiana University Press, 1990), 30–50.

38. I begin to pursue them in *Infant Figures* (Stanford, CA: Stanford University Press, 2000) by way of a meditation on the primal scene

Blanchot presents in *The Writing of the Disaster* (trans. Anne Smock [Lincoln: University of Nebraska Press, 1986]).

39. I develop this Benjaminian notion, and related terms such as "translatability" and "legibility," in *Language and Relation,* most specifically in the essay "The Claim of History," 211–25. While Benjamin's thought on language is infrequently addressed in a consequent fashion in the secondary literature, it remains the case that it lies at the heart of almost all his thinking. Running like a thread through his work, from beginning to end, is a meditation on the way language offers relation (each of the terms I have cited can be identified as instances of what he names, in "The Task of the Translator," *Relationsbegriffe,* "concept of relation"). As I try to demonstrate in the chapter to which I have referred, its most powerful sociopolitical articulation comes in "Konvolut N" of the *Passagen-Werk* when Benjamin envisions what we might call a writing of the present.

40. This comes in Wittgenstein's famous "Lecture on Ethics," which I take up in the opening pages of *Language and Relation.*

41. Jean-François Lyotard takes this tack when he opposes a thought of infancy—a placeholder for "the human"—to the inhuman forces of capital and *Technik* in *The Inhuman: Reflections on Time,* trans. Geoffrey Bennington and Rachel Bowlby (Stanford, CA: Stanford University Press, 1988).

42. In this essay, Heidegger argues that it is precisely the existence of the work, its reality—manifested in the way it presents that fact *that it is*—that gives access to a thought of the "thingly" character of a thing (what I have referred to generally with the phrase "material being"). Heidegger's strong statement in this regard has been underappreciated, in my view, as has his meditation on what he calls "earth." (Heidegger's statement on thingness comes late in the essay: "The fact that we never know thingness directly, and if we know it at all, then only vaguely and thus require the work—this fact proves indirectly that in the work's work-being the happening of truth, the opening up or disclosure of what is, is at work" [in *Poetry, Language, Thought,* trans. Albert Hofstadter (New York: Harper and Row, 1971), 70].) I would also recall that the "that" to which Heidegger refers has a fundamentally linguistic being. The essence of art is *Dichtung,* Heidegger says, and the essence of the latter is language. Of bodily experience, or the experience of the earth, Heidegger would insist that we say *es gibt,* not "it is." These notions are further developed in Heidegger's essay "The Essence of Language," in *On the Way to Language.*

I couple Heidegger's thinking of the way language gives relation to the earth with Blanchot's meditation on literary language and the *il y a* (which is a somewhat radicalized—that is to say, more abyssal—understanding of Heidegger's *es gibt*). For the "material" character of the *il y a*, one should consult Blanchot's "Literature and the Right to Death" (collected in *The Station Hill Blanchot Reader*, trans. Lydia Davis [Barrytown, NY: Station Hill Press, 1999], 359–99). I have found these meditations on language and materiality indispensable for the step I try to make in this volume in asserting that the humanities may address one of their essential concerns (the experience of material being) via language. Lyotard's meditation on bodily being took many forms in his career, but in the later years, it crystallized in his thought on infancy and something he termed "the unconscious body." I take up this issue in "Jean-François' Infancy," in *Yale French Studies*, no. 99 (2001): 44–61.

43. In a reading of Luce Irigaray's "La mystérique," in *Language and Relation* (161–74), I approach these topics, though I believe they require far more development. Irigaray's contributions for a thought of mimesis (like that developed by Philippe Lacoue-Labarthe) have not been sufficiently appreciated. I would turn also to Maurice Blanchot's meditations on the *fascinating* dimensions of literary language and art for this topic (see "Literature and the Right to Death" for far-reaching remarks on language and the imagination), and texts such as Blanchot's *The Madness of the Day* and *Thomas the Obscure* (also collected in *The Station Hill Blanchot Reader*) for an exploration of the mythopoieic dimensions of language.

44. The late Sarah Kofman provides profound testimony to this ethical relation that exceeds any relation of political power in *Smothered Words* (trans. Madeleine Dobie [Evanston, IL: Northwestern University Press, 1998]). The volume begins with testimony of her father's death at Auschwitz and then pursues a commentary on Maurice Blanchot's "The Idyll" and Robert Anthelme's *L'espèce humaine*. Kofman tries to bring to language again the "true speech" to which Blanchot points in his own commentary on Anthelme's crucial work—a language inseparable from the infinite, silent presence of the human other: "And yet, even in this situation of the most abject distress . . . where all that existed, even on the level of language, were relations of force and power, it was still possible, if only on rare occasions, to give voice to that which power cannot measure and which does not express any form of mastery, the relation without relation in which the other *(autrui)* is revealed" (51). (Blanchot, I would add, has argued that this speech is present in every act of speech, though it is rarely brought to language as such.) I take these words as one path for answering the contemporary assumption that "everything is political."

I cannot read her moving meditation on the possible meaning of humanism and community without recalling her manner of receiving a guest in her own intellectual community. From personal experience, I want to note that everything her text might suggest about the true meaning of hospitality was manifested in her actions. I thank Jessica Datema for calling my attention to this volume written at precisely the time I had the experience to which I allude.

45. This question—which is not just rhetorical—might be very profitably pursued through a careful response to Joan Scott's important essay "Experience" (in *Feminists Theorize the Political*, ed. Judith Butler and Joan W. Scott [New York: Routledge, 1992], 22–40). I am deeply sympathetic with Scott's critical treatment of the appeal to experience in traditional historical inquiry in this essay, and no less supportive of her nonfoundational approach to the discursive constitution of identities and experience. I also applaud her sense of what a "literary" approach can contribute to historical research. But I do not think that the model of the discursive constitution of subjectivity to which she points can account for the dimension of communication I am seeking to honor in evoking the exposure of the human. It seems clear to me that her important work must be supplemented by a consideration of linguistic experience at this latter level (a step with and beyond Foucault to the question of what is given in language with language itself). Only from there can one think the anarchic grounds of the ethicopolitical relation and the materiality of existence. Literary thought allows us to go further in thinking what language gives of material experience and the dimension of human freedom. Let me recognize, however, that Scott's treatment of these questions offers a salutary corrective to anything in my essay that would lend to a hypostatization or essentialization of human experience (in the most widely used sense of "essentialization"). I must emphasize that human freedom is always a *finite* transcendence, and must be thought in its always singular, material sites.

46. Lawrence Venuti develops this range of concerns forcefully in *The Scandals of Translation*. I have found Antoine Berman's book *The Experience of the Foreign* (trans. S. Heyvaert [Albany: State University of New York Press, 1992]) also vital for this topic, and have learned a great deal from Naoki Sakai's work on issues related to language and culture, most recently his *Translation and Subjectivity* (Minneapolis: University of Minnesota Press, 1997).

47. Heidegger insisted on this point throughout his work. It appears, for example, in the existential analytic when he insists that the Dasein cannot be an object of study, and then again in the meditations on language.

In "The Nature of Language" (in German, "Das Wesen der Sprache") Heidegger insists that Western thought has failed to think what speaks in the term *Logos* and has not met the challenge of thinking the relation between essence and the essence of language. Consequently, philosophy has not thought the manner in which essence is *given* in a mode of presencing that does not surrender to objectification. The assertion that we must learn to think without reference to things must be understood, I believe, in relation to this latter argument.

48. One might consult here Blanchot's meditation on Kafka's phrase "He was looking out the window" in "Literature and the Right to Death," or his own questioning relation to the piece of writing he introduces as "(A primal scene?)" in *The Writing of the Disaster*. I would also refer the reader to Jean-François Lyotard's attention to Walter Benjamin's writing in *Berliner Kindheit* (I take up this issue in "Jean-François' Infancy"). For literature of testimony such as that of Primo Levi, I would argue that it is imperative to attend to the modalities of writing contained in a text such as *Survival at Auschwitz* (and Levi's struggle with this question in the same text).

My reference to "stammering" hearkens back to Gilles Deleuze's development of this notion in *Dialogues,* with Claude Parnet (New York: Columbia University Press, 1987): "I should like to say what a style is. It belongs to people of whom you normally say, 'They have no style.' This is not a signifying structure, nor a reflected organization, nor a spontaneous inspiration, nor a little piece of music. It is an assemblage, an assemblage of enunciation. A style is managing to stammer in one's own language. It is difficult, because there has to be a need for such stammering. Not being a stammerer in one's speech, but being a stammerer of language itself" (4). And then the marvelous addition: "Life is like that too. In life there is a sort of awkwardness, a delicacy of health, a frailty of constitution, a vital stammering which is one's charm" (5).

49. The terms in quotation marks are borrowed, once again, from Walter Benjamin.

50. See, for this appeal to a "perhaps," Rodolphe Gasché's "Perhaps: A Modality," in *Of Minimal Things* (Stanford, CA: Stanford University Press, 1999), 173–91. I take up the same topic in *Language and Relation, 57–59,* reading Heidegger's notion of *Vermutung* as a kind of presumption. Jacques Derrida addresses it in the second chapter of *Politiques de l'amitié* (Paris: Galilée, 1994), 43–66, and throughout *L'université sans condition.*

51. This phrase appears in the "Fiche de lecture" of *Le différend* (Paris: Minuit, 1983), 10 (*The Differend,* xii).

52. My strongest experience of the meaning of this task came in a seminar that I codirected for several years with my colleague Bill Haver, then from the History Department at Binghamton. By teaming up to address topics of wide theoretical interest, we drew an extremely wide constituency and were forced to shape our language and methods accordingly. Facing students who did not share a common set of disciplinary assumptions (and facing each other), we could not rely on the usual intimacy of the seminar situation and were forced into a form of public presentation that remained a constant challenge.

53. Gilles Deleuze and Michel Foucault, "Les intellectuals et le pouvoir," *L'Arc,* no. 45 (1972): 3–10.

54. I have devoted much of this essay to research, but as I approach the end, I want to underscore the link from which I started: the relations between the humanities and the larger pedagogical ends they serve. Already in the Rockefeller report a lament is offered concerning the neglect into which the issue of education has fallen in discussion and debate within the humanities (though the fundamental assumptions governing the role of the humanities in education and the nature of their service to civic ideals is unshaken; for the authors of the report, the American government and society have failed the humanities—fewer criticisms are directed to those working in the fields of the humanities). But compare the situation today. What are we to make of the virtual nonexistence of discussion regarding the pedagogical mission of the humanities in theoretically informed debate, or of the status of teaching itself in "higher" education? What do we make of the fact that scholars in the humanities are not drawn to teaching if it is not in a form that reproduces the advanced seminars of their graduate study? I force the point slightly, but I have been astounded to observe that teaching has never been a viable answer (among the many needed) to the job crisis in the humanities that extends back at least to the time of the inception of the report. There are crucial societal factors at play here, of course, but I cannot help but suspect that the disconnection between study in the humanities and the act of teaching says a great deal about the vitality of the humanities themselves. What has happened to the humanities that teaching is not linked to their very idea? Can we conceive of research in the humanities, in the academy, apart from the structure of pedagogical exchange and a pedagogical mission?

55. Ota Yoko, *City of Corpses,* in *Hiroshima: Three Witnesses,* ed. and trans. Richard Minear (Princeton, NJ: Princeton University Press, 1990).

56. I believe I have brought this point home most strongly through the analysis of *City of Corpses,* a text first brought to my attention by

Bill Haver's powerful reading of it in *The Body of This Death: Historicity and Sociality in the Time of AIDS* (Stanford, CA: Stanford University Press, 1996), 74–118. In the course of her effort to write a historical record of her experience of the atomic bomb in Hiroshima (an effort carried out in the most extreme conditions and guided by the exigency to bring forth "a concrete piece of writing that was something less than literature and that crippled my zest for writing other works" [150]), Ota declares that she has discovered the "true form" of a "simple life": "That experience of living for three days on the riverbed among all those corpses, horrible as it was, left me as a human being with a profound and unique lesson that I shall never forget. Lives hinged on whether one had evacuated to a safe place before August 6. One speaks of the simple life, but I have a sense that now I have grasped its true form" (270). It is not clear that she is able to articulate for herself precisely what this means, but an attentive reading suggests that she is offering a thought of radical contingency. (Oddly enough, very few students initially catch this point in the very three sentences I have quoted; the parataxis in this passage somehow blocks their view.) In the page that follows her declaration, a page partly devoted to the point that the Japanese were enslaved by possessions prior to the time of the cataclysm, she argues that something of "Japan" has remained after the defeat: "But Japan and the Japanese belong to the Japanese; they cannot belong to anyone else" (271). Is this relation a possession? In the next paragraph, she then writes: "Most Japanese don't really seem to know what democracy is. But in order for Japan and the Japanese to revive or, better, in order to shed the old skin and carve out an image of a new human being, we have no alternative but to clear the way for democracy." Then, a little farther on the same page: "For the sake of true peace in the distant future, we must achieve a precise understanding of what needs doing right now; the fact that there will be deep suffering we must take for granted. . . . The somber reminder that we have a common fate absolutely forbids us to indulge in either nihilism or easy evasion." I have not yet achieved a satisfactory understanding of how Ota's thought is evolving through these lines, nor have I been able to deal adequately as yet with the question of translation (beyond keeping it in the foreground for the students), but I can say that discussions of the meaning of terms such as "contingency," "peace," "Japan and the Japanese," and "democracy," in the context of the difficult testimony contained in *City of Corpses,* have provided some of the richest experiences I have known in the classroom. I hope that this example can suggest that what I am trying to say about an experience with language cannot be reduced to any kind of formalism or aestheticism.

57. I would insist again that assuming such a task also means fighting for the institutional structures that permit such pedagogical relations to unfold.

58. One finds such an effort throughout Gérard Granel's later work. What distinguishes this effort is the thorough confrontation with the forces of modern capital.

59. To return to Hardt and Negri's *Empire,* I should dot the *i*'s and note that I am taking a position sharply divergent from theirs. Indeed, their discursive stance (which is that of transcendental subjects) is diametrically opposed to the "local" one I am describing. Because there is virtually no thought of language in this volume (beyond an undeveloped concept of communication), and thus no challenge to the order of representation, their intervention can only be regressive in a politico-philosophical sense. Their claim to be writing beyond metaphysics is hard to fathom given their discursive stance and the metaphysical character of many of their theses.

For a more rigorous questioning of local thinking, one might consider Wendy Brown's argument for the necessity of theory in *States of Injury* ("While what have come to be called postmodern epistemological and ontological insights commission political claims of a partial, situated and local character, the development of an emancipatory or radically democratic politics within contemporary political conditions requires incessant theorization of these conditions and, at times at least, an accounting of their global movement" [31]). She also provides a most supple understanding of how such theorizing might proceed. I subscribe to much of her argument, but I reiterate again that a thought that proceeds from the humanities must find ways to honor events that are always of a local, or singular, character. I am also inclined to think that we must accept the risk, in the humanities, of not always knowing the political implications of our thinking. (The late Francis Bacon's reflections in this regard seem important here.) In general, I would say that we must learn to think the supplemental relation between the forms of engagement I have described in this essay and the kinds of important theoretical movements evoked by Brown.

60. I believe that Gayatri Spivak points to such a notion in her reference to what she calls "open-plan fieldwork"—a form of activity that is prepared by her research (in literary study, language study, and theoretical work), but quite escapes any academic and commodifying framework. I have tried to convey to my students that work in the humanities can prepare individuals to *go out* toward innumerable sites. Spivak's experience in West Bengal speaks dramatically to this phenomenon, and I can

say that I have glimpsed something of it myself in the American inner city. In an essay for *Vacarme* ("Peut-on être citoyen d'un empire?" *Vacarme,* no. 8 [Winter 2002]: 18–20), I tried to suggest that such a mode of exposure might be critical for thinking the possibility of community even in America (my example was Bedford-Stuyvesant, Brooklyn, where the question is confronted every day across class, racial, and linguistic boundaries).

Index

Christopher Fynsk is professor of comparative literature and philosophy at Binghamton University. He is the author of *Infant Figures: The Death of the "Infans" and Other Scenes of Origin, Language and Relation: . . . that there is language,* and *Heidegger: Thought and Historicity.*